GARDENING WISDOM

TIME-PROVEN SOLUTIONS FOR TODAY'S
GARDENING CHALLENGES

DOUGLAS GREEN

THE CONTEMPORARY GARDENER

CONTEMPORARY BOOKS

Library of Congress Cataloging-in-Publication Data

Green, Douglas.
    Gardening wisdom: time-proven solutions for
today's gardening challenges / Douglas Green.
        p.   cm.
    Includes bibliographical references (p.).
    ISBN 0-8092-2527-1
    1. Gardening.   I. Title.
SB455.G69   2000
635—dc21   99-55648

THE CONTEMPORARY GARDENER
Other books in the Contemporary Gardener series:
Growing Perennials in Cold Climates, *Mike Heger and John Whitman*
Growing Roses in Cold Climates, *Jerry Olson and John Whitman*
The Landscaping Revolution, *Andy Wasowski and Sally Wasowski*
Gaining Ground, *Maureen Gilmer*

Interior design by Kim Bartko
Illustrations from the author's collection except as noted
Illustrations on pages 19, 44, 68, 74, 83, 112, 120 by Dan Krovatin

Published by Contemporary Books
A division of NTC/Contemporary Publishing Group, Inc.
4255 West Touhy Avenue, Lincolnwood (Chicago), Illinois 60712-1975 U.S.A.
Copyright © 2000 by Douglas Green
Printed in Canada
International Standard Book Number: 0-8092-2527-1
00 01 02 03 04 05 TCP 19 18 17 16 15 14 13 12 11 10 9 8 7 6 5 4 3 2 1

TO ROBERT

So that when he has finished putting balls into hoops, he can
look back and remember what he was taught

Contents

Acknowledgments

ANDREA. My inspiration, who somehow knows where I want to go and gave me my first old book many years ago.

MY GARDENING PREDECESSORS. I owe them much more than I can ever repay. Part payment is in remembering and honoring their work. Each of the people referenced in the book taught me something and together they have changed the way I garden.

JEANNE FREDERICKS, my agent, for her ever-patient self.

THE FOLKS AT Contemporary Books, for the courage to take on this project and carry it through.

Introduction:
Wherein the Author Has His Say

EN SUPRA VITA FUGAX EN

INFRA CERTA MORS

A life on flight's soon out of sight.

—A Book of Sundial Mottoes

ooks—old books have become the gardening grandparents I never had. The information in them is a true mix of the kind of lore grandparents have been handing down for years. Some of it is good, solid advice and some . . . well, some is a bit out of date. I started collecting old gardening books just as something to do and for the curiosity of the information they contained. Their unique voices have since become my entry point into an exclusive world of bygone skills and attitudes. These authors speak of the changes in our gardens: changes in the plants, the techniques and the very way in which we approach this activity we call gardening. They speak across the years of a very high regard—one might even call it love—of the soil and the gardening lifestyle it enables. As I tuck myself into bed or put my feet up on my desk and share a few moments with an author who is long since dead, I feel a sense of continuity and clearly hear his or her voice as it struggles to describe not only the techniques of growing things but also the intangibles that only fellow gardeners understand.

These techniques and intangibles have led me to collect ever more old gardening books, to search through dusty corners and out-of-the-way places to find the treasures that speak to me of gardening in voices from my past. Indeed, if you are a gardener, these voices are from your past as well. All those of us who garden share in this continuity of knowledge, just as we share in the continuity of plants. We pass along our plants from neighbor to neighbor and think of that as a normal part of gardening; so, too, we transmit techniques to one another across backyard fences and down through the years.

One tragedy of gardening is that often this wisdom is lost or bent in the translation. Voices that start out so clear and resolute are forgotten, lost, or consigned to the back shelf to sit, molding and sad, victims of progress. Often lost along with them are the techniques that produced their garden bounty. In these pages, I intend to pass along some of the authors' words as well as their gardening advice.

Some of the techniques are extremely valuable and deserve to be remembered. Some might better be mentioned and stored away again, while others will undoubtedly produce laughter when exposed to the harsh glare of modern research. Whatever the value of their methods, what should not be forgotten is the essence that compelled each of these people to write about gardening. In these books, we hear the voices of real gardeners.

For example, in the introduction to his *Gardening for Profit* ([1866] 1895), Peter Henderson writes, "I hope it is no egotism to state that in both the Floral and Vegetable departments of

Horticulture, in which I have been engaged for the past eighteen years, I have been entirely successful. From this standpoint, I claim the right to attempt the instruction of the student of horticulture in the tactics in the field." No mealymouthed statements here; this is one author who claims his knowledge is up to snuff, and so it is.

On the other hand, Jane Loudon is a touch more humble in her introduction to her classic *Gardening for Ladies and Companion to the Flower Garden* ([1843] 1851): "When I married Mr. Loudon, it is scarcely possible to imagine a person more completely ignorant than I was, of every thing relating to plants and gardening; and, as may be easily imagined, I found every one about me so well acquainted with the subject, that I was soon heartily ashamed of my ignorance. My husband, of course, was quite as anxious to teach me as I was to learn, and it is the result of his instructions that I now (after ten years experience of their efficacy) wish to make public for the benefit of others."

It should be noted that not only was Mr. Loudon one of England's more famous writers on the garden, but Mrs. Loudon's name did not appear on the cover of the American edition of her book. Rather, the name of A. J. Downing, a well-known American plantsman, was listed as the editor of the work on the spine. Perhaps the publicity department of the publisher took Mrs. Loudon's modesty to heart.

Frank J. Scott, in the groundbreaking American book, *Beautiful Homes* ([1870] 1886), put it directly: "The aim of this book is to aid persons of moderate income, who know little of the arts of decorative gardening, to beautify their homes; to suggest and illustrate the simple means with which beautiful home-surroundings may be realized on small grounds, and with little cost; and thus to assist in giving an intelligent direction to the desires, and a satisfactory result for the labors of those who are engaged in embellishing homes, as well as those whose imaginations are warm with the hopes of homes that are yet to be." Well, perhaps not as directly as we might write today, but his voice from 1870 still sounds clear to my ear. I consider myself of moderate income and would welcome his suggestions for beautifying my home "with little cost."

Some wrote to express a viewpoint on the state of landscape design, such as did William Robinson, one of the most influential of garden writers of the late nineteenth century. He started the ninth edition of his influential *The English Flower Garden* (1905) with these words: "There was little or no reason admitted into garden design: the same poor imitation of the Italian garden being set down in all sorts of positions. If the place did not suit the style, the ground had to be bolstered up in some way so that the plan might be carried out—a costly way to get an often ridiculous result." Robinson's book is directly responsible for what we now call the English border or cottage-garden style of gardening. Historically, cottage-style gardening is the grandfather of the landscape style referred to as "New American," or simply "American," with its use of North American native plants.

Gardeners write for a variety of reasons. In 1879, John Macoun and H. B. Spotton wrote *The Elements of Structural*

Botany because, they explained, "The works on Botany, many of them of great excellence, which have found their way into this country, have been prepared with reference to climates differing, in some cases, very widely from our own."

Reginald Farrer, the great plant explorer and alpine gardener, began his classic *The English Rock Garden* ([1918] 1928) with these words: "Proclamations of purpose are often confessions of failure to achieve it." Farrer had a way with words and was never faint of heart when expressing an opinion.

The reader will be the judge of the proclamations of this book. If the gardening methods and information are worthy, then the book will be judged accordingly. If not, Farrer will have had the last word, as he so often did in life.

A LOVE AFFAIR IN THE GARDEN

With whom did he fall in love? Rose Geranium

Was she handsome? An American Beauty

Did she have many admirers? Phlox

What was his name? Basil

How did he propose? Aster

What time of day was their first meeting? Morning Glory

What was the color of her eyes? Violet

What was the color of her cheeks? Pink

What did he wear upon his hands? Fox Gloves

What fastened his coat? Bachelor Buttons

What had she upon her feet? Lady Slippers

Her parents were worldly and what had she been told to do?
    Marigold

What did her lover offer her? Tulips

What was the result? Love in a Tangle

Faithful to her parents' commands, what did she say?
    Touch me not

What did he say, pleading with her? Honeydew

What did she hope would efface their love? Thyme

He fell down upon his knees before her and what did she say
    to him? Johnny-jump-up

What did he do? Rose

What did they both have when they parted? Bleeding Hearts

What did he think of becoming? Monkshood

What did she think of becoming? Veiled Nun

When, after many months the parents relented, what did the
    lovers find? Sweet Peas

What hour was set for the wedding? Four O'clock

Who was the best man? Sweet William

What did the mother say to the bride? Forget-me-not

Where did they make their home? Cape Jessamine

What did they find in married life? Heartsease

    —LINUS WOOLVERTON, ED., *The Canadian Horticulturalist*

CHAPTER ONE

SOILS

OMNES VOS FILII LUCIS ESTIS ACFILII
DIEI NON SUMUS FILII NOCTIS NEQUE
TENEBRARUM

*Ye are all the children of light and the children of the
day; we are not of the night nor the darkness.*

—A BOOK OF SUNDIAL MOTTOES

igging and spading—preparing the soil—
is hard work. The modern myth of gardening is that we can substitute boxed
fertilizers for the work, and then simply
get on with our gardening and our lives. However, when I read
the old authors, the very first thing that becomes crystal clear is
the emphasis they place on the soil and its preparation. We have
lost that emphasis in our modern garden practices and writing,
preferring instead the instant gratification of design, bloom, and
color. The more I garden, the more I become aware of just how
right these authors really are: get the soil conditions correctly
established and the design, bloom, and color of the plants will
follow. In 1629, John Parkinson wrote, "that the lesse rich or
more baren that your ground is, there needeth the more care,
labour and cost to bee bestowed thereon, both to order it rightly,
& so to preserve it from time to time" (Parkinson [1629] 1927). It
was clearly understood even then that the garden soil had to be
"ordered rightly" if the garden was to be a success. How can we

do less than that demanded by the Botanicus Regius Primarius (King's Head Gardener) to Charles I of England?

You must understand, You must understand, that the lesse rich or more baren that your ground is, there needeth the more care, labour and cost to bee bestowed thereon, both to order it rightly, & so to preserve it from time to time: for no artificiall or forc't ground can endure good any long time, but that within a few years it must be refreshed more or lesse, according as it dothe require.

— JOHN PARKINSON, *A Garden of Pleasant Flowers*

How then do we "order rightly" our soils? How do we create those wonderful soils on which to base our dreams?

It is most interesting to compare the methods of yesterday with the methods of today. One comes to the conclusion that our predecessors knew almost as much as we do, and that the cultivation of a garden has changed very little in its fundamental wisdom. We may have advanced in certain scientific aspects, but in the everyday business, we have little to teach our forebears.

— VITA SACKVILLE-WEST, *More for Your Garden*

We start at the beginning, by understanding just how soils are structured. When we know how a soil *should* work, it becomes infinitely easier to modify or "order rightly" the soil we have inherited. It is comforting to understand that you are not alone in this struggle to deal with poor soil. Gardeners before you have worked long and hard to pass along the lessons you'll put to good practice, and the basics haven't changed all that much. What these forebears can teach us is that great gardeners have a loving relationship with their soil. They understand, sometimes intuitively, that this ongoing relationship is very much like a good love affair. There is give and take on both sides, but ultimately its success depends on a willingness to totally commit one's energies to understanding and meeting the real needs of the other. Vita Sackville-West (1955) put it this way: "The principle, however, is always the same: you cannot expect your soil and your plants to go on giving you of their best if you are not prepared to give something back in return. This is as true of gardens as of human relationships." What is clear in the history of gardening is that both the soil and the spirit of the garden are ready to make the commitment as soon as the gardener screws up the courage to do the same.

SOIL COMPONENTS

While our gardening predecessors may have referred to "primitive earths" and "silex," we now know that garden soil is composed of three mineral particles of differing sizes: sands (which range in size from 2 mm to .1 mm), silt particles (from .05 to .002 mm), and clay particles (smaller than .002 mm in size). The proportion of these particles in a soil determines the textural name of the soil. For example, if a soil has more than 30 percent clay particles, it is called clay. Scientists classify soils into many different groups; all based on their proportions of sand, silt, and clay. In later sections, the reader will be given clear directions for modifying soils by using some of these different-sized particles.

ALL THE DIFFERENT KINDS of soil found on level ground consist of two parts, which are called the surface-soil and the sub-soil; and as the sub-soil always consists of one of the three primitive earths, so do these earths always enter, more or less, into the composition of every kind of surface soil. The primitive earths are silex (which includes sand and gravel), clay and lime, which includes also chalk; and most sub-soils consist of a solid bed or rock of one or other of these materials, probably in nearly the same state as it was left by the deluge.

— JANE LOUDON, *Gardening for Ladies and Companion to the Flower Garden*

Another soil component that is extremely important to practical gardeners is humus, decomposing organic matter that coats and holds the mineral pieces in place to form soil aggregates. From a practical gardening point of view, humus is the most important component of the soil mix, and its creation and use is described in more detail below.

The relative proportions of these soil components determine the all-important soil texture. Texture in turn determines the absorption rate of water, how much water will be stored for future use, the ease of tilling, and how much oxygen can be stored in the soil to be utilized by growing plant roots. A clay soil, one composed of more than 30 percent clay particles, resists water penetration because the soil particles fit so tightly together, so once in between the clay particles, water is not easily moved or drained. Soil composed of bigger particles, such as sand, has larger openings between the particles, which admit water more easily and allow it to move downward — sometimes too quickly. Good garden soil has to have a combination of these two characteristics; the soil must admit and store water, but it must also allow free drainage in overly wet conditions. The ease of working a soil is also directly influenced by its composition. Soils with smaller particles are dense, while soils with larger particles are looser. Any experience at all with a shovel will convince a gardener that open spaced soils are lighter and easier to work. This difficulty of working clay soils is one reason they are often referred to as "heavy" soils.

Too MUCH EMPHASIS cannot be laid on the importance of porosity. We remember once hearing Mr. Grove say that the ideal soil should be "frothy" — an admirable word — should be such that "you can thrust your arm into it as far as the elbow."

— H. DRYSDALE WOODCOCK, K.C.; AND J. COUTTS, V.M.H.

No MAN WILL DENY, but the naturall blacke mould is not only the fattest and richest, but farre exceedeth any other either naturall or artificiall, as well in goodness as durability. And next thereunto, I hold the sandy loame (which is light and yet firme, but not so loose as sand, nor stiffe like unto clay) to be little inferior for this our Garden of Pleasure. But of all other sorts of grounds, the stiffe clay is the very worst.

— JOHN PARKINSON, *A Garden of Pleasant Flowers*

The size of the spaces between particles also determines the ease with which oxygen moves into or around within the soil. Plant roots require oxygen for growth, and in clay soils, with their small spaces, oxygen has a hard time making itself available. This is particularly true in wet seasons or in the spring, when water fills all available spaces in the clay. Heavy clay soils do not support early spring plant growth as well as the more open sandy soils do.

Each kind of soil extreme has positive as well as negative characteristics. What gardeners all want is deep, well-aerated, moisture-holding yet well-draining, highly organic soil. Such a soil is the stuff of our dreams.

For although you should digge out the whole compasse of your Garden, carry it away, and bring other good mould in the stead thereof, and fill up the place, yet the nature of that clay is so predominant, that in a small time it will eate out the heart of the good mould, and convert it to its owne nature, or very neare unto it.

—John Parkinson, *A Garden of Pleasant Flowers*

Dream we might, but all of the above information is of little consequence to you unless the techniques of modifying and improving the soil can be incorporated into your gardening practices. If for a moment you return to the first quotation of this chapter, you will see that John Parkinson also says "to preserve it from time to time." This means that not only must the gardener get the soil properly established to begin a garden, there is also ongoing work involved "to preserve it from time to time . . . as it doth require" (Parkinson [1629] 1907). The following sections describe the practical considerations that we need to address and, I might add, that have been addressed by our gardening forebears.

Humus

Humus is simply organic matter, both of plant and animal origin, in an advanced stage of decomposition. Even once reaching this advanced stage, organic matter continues to decompose into its chemical components and plays a vitally important role in feeding our soils due to its cation exchange capacity. Cation exchange capacity, or CEC, refers to a chemical reaction important in creating and maintaining soil fertility, in modifying and maintaining soil acidity ranges, and in modifying our soils' physical properties such as drainage and water-holding capacity. In a very small nutshell, cations are used by the roothairs of a plant as a food source. Once absorbed by the plant, these used-up cations are replaced ("exchanged") with new cations on the surfaces of the root hairs. The relative ability of different materials to accomplish this exchange gives us the further term "capacity." Humus, in its final stages of decomposition, has an extremely high cation exchange capacity, and is thus a great food source. While scientists don't totally understand this process at the molecular level, gardeners seem to instinctively know that organic matter will rot down into humus and, when it is decomposed enough, this humus will become available as food to our plant friends. Even before it is decomposed enough to be food it acts as a soil binder and acidity moderator, and, in larger, less decomposed states, it also serves as a soil particle separator to increase drainage in clay soils or as a water-holding agent in sandy soils.

HORSE MANURE IS for stiff and cold ground; sheeps for hot and dry; ashes for cold, stiff and moist; old woolen rags for poor and dry; lyme is most excellent for moorish and heathy land; hair of beasts for dry and stiff ground; pigeons and poultrie-manure for cold and moist; rotten saw dust for dry; rubbish of buildings for stiff cold grounds; salt for cold and moist but use it moderately, for it destroys vegetables on dry ground, especially at first, but when melted by winter rains, it fertilizeth."

—JOHN REID, *The Scots Gard'ner*

FEEDING THE SOIL: ORGANIC MATTER AS LIFEBLOOD

Decaying organic matter is the lifeblood of our soil. Feed the soil, not the plants, is a common dictum in the environmental or organic gardening literature. By creating a good soil, with excellent organic matter and good fertility, you ensure that plants will grow well. Most gardeners today use compost as their source of organic matter, but while they apply compost to all parts of their garden, they don't live up to the standards set by most of our gardening predecessors, either in quantity or quality.

One question that I am often asked is, "How much compost should be applied to the average garden?" Peter Henderson ([1866] 1895), who wrote the classic *Gardening for Profit*, advises, "Of stable or barnyard manure, from fifty to one hundred tons per acre is used, and prepared, for at least six months previously, by thoroughly turning and breaking up to prevent its heating unduly." An acre contains 43,560 square feet. If we divide the compost to be applied by the area, we obtain an amount of approximately four and a half pounds of compost to the square foot at his highest recommended application rate.

This could be cut in half to two pounds to the square foot to meet this expert's minimum requirements. Beginning gardeners also question whether they have to apply this compost every year. I will let Mr. Henderson ([1866] 1895) answer for the both of us: "I never yet saw soil of any kind that had borne a crop of vegetables that would produce as good a crop the next season without the use of manure, no matter how 'rich' the soil may be thought to be." To that I can only add that the same holds true for the general flower border as well. Apply compost heavily and regularly every spring.

THESE SPECIAL FERTILIZERS for special crops are gradually increasing in number, so that some dealers now offer fifty kinds, different brands being offered for plants belonging to the same family. There is an ignorant assumption in this, and any cultivator of ordinary intelligence cannot fail to see that the motive in so doing is to strike as broad a swath as possible, so that a larger number of customers may be reached and a higher price obtained.

— PETER HENDERSON, *Gardening for Profit*

As a nurseryman and writer, I'm often asked by salesmen to sell or test their special fertilizers. Every reader will have seen these specialty packages in their garden center, one for just about every kind of plant or flower. My own experience is that the plants do not seem to know the difference between these specialty fertilizers and plain old compost. Use compost, and use lots of it. Find a way to make it or at the very least purchase it in suitable amounts for your garden.

THESE HAIR-SPLITTING DISTINCTIONS are not recognized to be of any value by one practical farmer or gardener in a hundred; for a little experience soon shows that pure bone dust or well-rotted stable manure answers for all crops nearly alike, no matter what they are.

—PETER HENDERSON, *Gardening for Profit*

Manure or Compost Tea

Many gardeners think the use of compost tea is a recent discovery by the gardening community. (For the uninitiated, this tea is simply manure or compost dissolved in water, making nutrients more readily available to plants.) Thomas Mawe, in the early nineteenth century reported on an 1812 lecture given by the British chemist Sir Humphrey Davy to the British Board of Agriculture where he said, "Amongst excrementitious solid substances used as manures, one of the most powerful is the dung of birds that feed on animal food, particularly the dung of sea-birds." Davy went on to say, "It is easy to explain its fertilizing properties: from its composition it might be supposed to be a very powerful manure. *It requires water for the solution of its soluble matter*, to enable it to produce its full beneficial effect on crops" (Mawe and Abercrombie n.d.). (Italics in original.)

For GROUND CULTURE, we would suggest the guano be always used in conjunction with some other spent manures, and not alone unless applied as a liquid manure in dry weather, when one ounce *stirred up* in three gallons of pond water, will prove very available.

—THOMAS MAWE AND JOHN ABERCROMBIE, *The Complete Gardener*

At our farm, I put several shovels of compost into a porous old sack and dunk it into a five-gallon pail of water. When the water turns brown, I immediately apply it directly to the plants without fear of burning or harming new growth. Once the filled bag will no longer give brown tea, I empty the spent compost onto the garden where it will further decay and enrich the soil. In this way, immediate results from the liquid feeding are obtained (plant leaves will change color overnight if they are in a starved condition), and the benefits of soil organic matter are retained by applying the spent organic matter to the ground. I am often asked how much compost to add to the sack and I have to confess that, as this is not rocket science, I rarely measure accurately, preferring instead to put a few indeterminate shovels full into the sack depending on how strongly I feel about carrying it back to the garden. (Our compost pile is several hundred feet from our front gardens.) Heavily loaded sacks do not fit into the pail easily and it is better to work with too little than have compost tea sloshing about your ankles. I aim to apply compost tea to my annual and rose garden areas once a week; this boosts flowering performance in ways that must be seen to be believed. As a realistic gardener and honest author, I note my composting is not always at the once-a-week level I would like it to be.

ALL SOIL, TO BE in a fit state for growing plants, should be sufficiently loose and dry to allow of passing through it intermixed with air; as water, when in this state, is never more than slightly impregnated with the nutritious juices of the manure through which it has passed.

—JANE LOUDON, *Gardening for Ladies and Companion to the Flower Garden*

Other gardeners share my enthusiasm for the effects of manure tea on flower blooms as is seen in that earlier this century, in her garden diary on June 18, Mrs. Francis King wrote, "The applying of liquid manure is a vast help toward getting finer flowers and this is the time to give it to the plants in limited quantities. About a bushel of manure in a burlap bag should be hung in a barrel of water for some days. If this solution is weak it can be poured around plants twice a week, but if strong, not so often" (King 1927). Gardeners can use their own compost, purchased compost, or bagged manure, but the secret is to add water, obtain a "nutritious juice," and pour it around your plants.

Green Manure and Other Organic Matter Sources

Some gardeners complain that they are not able to develop enough compost or organic matter for their gardens. Gardeners who are not able to make enough compost to properly feed their grounds can use "green manure" instead. This is an easy way to improve the organic matter component of soils. Various crops have been suggested by different authors, ranging from buckwheat right through to comfrey. All have their proponents, but it seems to me that the best ones are those that, if planted after a garden area is harvested, will make good growth before killing frosts. Also, plants for green manure should be annuals in your area, killed by winter temperatures so they do not in turn become weeds the next year. Even in my Zone 4 garden, it is not unusual to have some volunteer annual rye, oats, or buckwheat seeds overwinter and germinate. Had these been perennial plants, I'd be digging them out forever. There are two ways that green manure is used in gardens. The first is as a late-season crop planted after the vegetable crop has been harvested and then allowed to grow until a very late plowing or tilling. The second method is to rest a plot of ground for the summer. Instead of vegetables plant a green manure crop that can either be allowed to grow unimpeded all summer or regularly knocked down and replanted. Regularly knocking the green crop down by tilling and then reseeding it increases the amount of green foliage matter produced during the season, with the resulting increase in organic matter incorporated into the soil.

FOR HUMUS, WHERE MANURE is not available, sow a green crop, such as clover or rye, in the Fall, for digging in during Spring; or dig in lawn clippings, rotted compost, weeds or leaves between the rows during the Summer.

 —A.B. CUTTING, *Canadian Home Gardening the Year Round*

ADD DAILY TO THE compost heap all fallen leaves raked from the lawn. It cannot be too often said that one of the greatest of all wastes in gardening is the autumn burning of good leaves.

 —MRS. FRANCIS KING, *The Flower Garden Day by Day*

Others who may not have the inclination for green manuring, many of them perhaps city gardeners with small plots, would do well to listen to *Organic Gardening Magazine* (September 1948), in its "Garden Calendar": "During September and the following months, millions of tons of leaves will fall to the ground. Many of these leaves are rich in minerals that have been absorbed from the lower levels of the soil. They should be composted and returned to the soil and thus maintain all essential elements in the soil in sufficient amounts to meet the needs of the plants. Then and only then will our garden equal or even surpass the pictures in the seed catalogues."

Surpassing the pictures in seed catalogs is a fine target for any gardener.

PREPARING SOILS FOR PLANTING

Luckily, as gardeners we rarely need to be soil scientists. In our earthbound gardens, there are techniques and solutions that will allow the worst soil to produce blooms or edibles successfully. One thing that has constantly amazed me is the advice that some garden writers and horticultural leaders give that the only good way to get good soil is to purchase it and replace the existing garden soil. All too often I have heard customers at our nursery say that their soil had stopped producing so they replaced it. They actually dug out the soil in a large garden bed, putting in newly purchased soil in its place. The addition of good compost will bring almost any impoverished soil to life, and those who spend money on new soil when the old is not producing up to their dreams have more money than good gardening sense.

Digging

If we look at the bright side of garden digging, we can immediately see it is cheaper than belonging to a health club, can be done anytime rather than having to wait for an aerobics class to start, is done in the comfort and safety of your own garden, does not require fancy clothes, and has a fashion sense that is down-right relaxed. This is great exercise for young and old, it costs nothing, and it only resembles work in a peripheral sort of way. Planting a garden is also, as Charles Dudley Warner (1885) says, doing something for the good of the world, and improving the world begins with the first step: using a shovel.

HOWEVER SMALL IT IS on the surface, it is 4,000 miles deep; and that is a very handsome property. And there is a great pleasure in working in the soil, apart from the ownership of it. The man who has planted a garden feels that he has done something for the good of the world. He belongs to the producers.

— CHARLES DUDLEY WARNER, *My Summer in a Garden*

There are several things to bring to the attention of neo-phyte diggers. The most important of these is an ergonomic and health principle. Use the ball of the foot to push against the shovel, not the more instinctive instep. If the instep is used as the primary force against the metal edge of the shovel, repeated thrusts or sudden jarring impacts with rocks will stretch the foot tendons, creating a very painful and slow-healing condition. Wear stiff working shoes or boots when digging. At first using the ball of the foot for all thrusting motions with tools will seem awkward, but with practice and attention to this detail your body will quickly accept the new method, making it seem natural and easy.

GARDEN SPADE

The uses of digging having thus been explained, it is now necessary to say something of its practice, and particularly of its application to ladies. It must be confessed that digging appears at first sight a very laborious employment and one particularly unfitted to small and delicately formed hands and feet; but, by a little attention to the principles of mechanics and the laws of motion, the labour may be much simplified and rendered comparitively easy.

— Jane Loudon, *Gardening for Ladies and Companion to the Flower Garden*

The second point is to decide how much digging you want to accomplish. For this question there is no right answer. The following methods have been described by different gardeners over the years and will produce different results.

Single Digging

Single digging is the turning over of a garden and is generally used on existing garden beds in the years when you don't desire a full double digging. A simple turning of the soil is the absolute minimum attention any garden requires each spring. In alternate years, my kitchen garden is single dug. I find it easiest to spread the compost on top of the soil, and then begin digging the first trench across the bed and heaving the soil down to the other end of the bed. This annual process is one of the main reasons that none of my kitchen garden beds is longer than eight feet, just about the limit of an accurate heave with a shovel of soil. Once the first trench is dug to a depth of one shovel blade, approximately 9 inches or one spit in British terms, I begin the second trench and use the soil from that to fill in the first trench. This repetitive digging and filling creates its own rhythm as I work my way down the bed until the last trench is dug. I finish off the bed with a rake to level and give myself the aesthetic pleasure of seeing a perfect seedbed.

THE GROUND SHOULD BE dunged with some good rotten dung, and afterwards should be dug or trenched one spade deep; taking care to bury the dung in a regular manner at the bottom of the trench.

— THOMAS MAWE AND JOHN ABERCROMBIE, *The Complete Gardener*

Double Digging

Double digging is the kind of garden work that does two things to the average human being. First, it makes us aware of every screaming muscle that has not been used in the preceding twelve months; and second, it creates a special kind of warmth that only gardeners understand. While gardening may be the most satisfactory thing we do, digging is the most useful thing we can do. And our gardens reward us for it.

WHEN ANY SOIL, EXCEPT sand or loose gravel, remains unstirred for a length of time, it becomes hard and its particles adhere so firmly together as not to be separated without manual force. It is quite clear that when soil is in this state, it is unfit for the reception of seeds; as the tender roots of the young plants will not be able to penetrate it without great difficulty, and neither air nor water can reach them in sufficient quantity to make them thrive.

— JANE LOUDON, *Gardening for Ladies and Companion to the Flower Garden*

I use double digging for several specific purposes. The first is when I create a new garden bed. This full digging enables me to remove all the stones and weed roots that are sure to bedevil my garden and my efforts at growing the perfect flower. It also creates a perfectly aerated soil. Secondly, I double dig my kitchen garden beds every two years. These beds are intensively used and each one of these four-foot-by-eight-foot beds produces multiple crops of summer salads. This intensive growing is hard on the soil and I find that by adding in heavy amounts of compost during the digging, our yields of leafy salad crops double and the bitterness in the lettuce crop is reduced or eliminated. I also double dig the carrot bed every year. Carrots from a properly double-dug bed are a delight to behold. Our double-dug beds produce, instead of the twisted, stunted roots we get from our regular, stony ground, long, straight carrots with no stress lines or bitterness. The organic matter that I apply heavily during digging acts as a buffer during heat or dry spells, and the carrots respond to this evenness of water and temperature by growing long, straight, and sweet.

Nevertheless, what a man needs in gardening is a cast-iron back, with a hinge in it.

— Charles Dudley Warner, *My Summer in a Garden*

Double digging differs from single digging in that the depth of the trench is twice as deep. Two shovels deep is quite a bite to take out of a garden, but the creation of perfect topsoil to this depth is a gardener's dream. The first trench is dug and the soil is removed to the other end of the garden. I confess I often cheat at this stage and excavate the other end of the garden first. I take that soil and just throw it over the entire bed without trying to

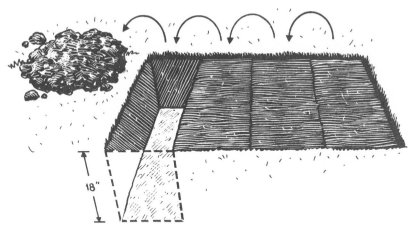

DOUBLE DIGGING

save it in any one specific spot. This gives me a hole in which to throw the soil from the trench I am supposed to dig first. If this sounds complicated, refer to the diagram above. While I excavate the first trench to a depth of 18 inches, I am constantly doing two things. First, I look for any weed roots and also pick out the rocks and pebbles I come across. Both of these waste items go into the wheelbarrow kept beside the bed. If not put into the wheelbarrow at this time, they make a huge messy pile beside the bed and are regularly "forgotten." Messy gardens equal messy minds and the older I get the more I have to work at keeping my garden neat. The second thing I do is improve my soil during digging by adding a shovel full of compost and a shovel of peat moss for every three shovels of original garden soil taken out. This, too, quickly becomes a rhythm in the garden: three shovels of soil, *whap*, *whap*, *whap*, shovel of peat, *whuff*, shovel of compost, *whump*, and I move on to the next digging. Once the first trench is excavated, as in single digging, the soil from the second trench is moved into the existing hole. Again, three shovels of soil are moved followed by a shovel of peat and a shovel of compost: *whap*, *whap*, *whap*, *whuff*, *whump*, all down the bed.

This digging creates soil to dream on. It is a wonderfully aerated and fed soil that will grow almost anything—especially sweet carrots.

SOLVING PROBLEMS WITH SOILS

IT IS ESSENTIAL TO STUDY the secret of the soil and find out the plants that thrive best on it. Once free from the limits and needs of the flower garden proper, the best way will often be to use any local peculiarities of soil instead of doing away with them: A bog? Instead of draining it keep it and adorn it with some of the often beautiful things that grow in bogs; A sandy knoll? Plant with Rosemary or Rock Roses; A peaty sheltered hollow? Make it into a beautiful rhododendron glade, and so get variety of plant life in various conditions.

—WILLIAM ROBINSON, *The English Flower Garden*

There are two approaches to solving problems with soils in the garden. The first is to learn to live with the soil that is already there and put plants in that like the existing natural conditions. However, in my experience two things are true of gardeners. We rarely want to grow the plants that grow best in our soils and we always want to grow plants that are too tender for our climate. Given the new millennium movement toward natural gardens, perhaps there is hope yet for growing the plants that will thrive in our natural garden soil. However, I believe there is faint hope of many serious gardeners ever desiring to grow *only* those plants that grow in their neighborhood. My own gardens have annual and perennial plants from six of the seven continents (Antarctica being the exception) and while the individual plant species may change from time to time, the diversity will not. So I, and I suspect the majority of gardeners, will ignore the sage advice of those recommending naturalized gardens and plunge headlong into the second approach to soil problem solving. That is, we modify our existing soil so that we may grow the plants of our choice. This modification at the simplest level is adding organic matter to improve the humus content, while more serious gardeners, such as alpine specialists, create special sand beds, peat beds, or gravel beds to house their treasures. Most of us, however, face one of two problems: too much clay or too much sand.

Too Much Clay

Heavy clay soils, while they might grow good roses, are the bane of serious perennial flower and vegetable gardeners. The problems stem from the small size of the constituent clay particles; all solutions involve separating these particles. By adding coarse material to the clay, we cause the individual clay particles to separate, allowing air and water to move more freely. This is the basic principle by which clay soils in the garden have been and still are amended.

BUT OF ALL OTHER SORTS of grounds, the stiffe clay is the very worst. . . . So that to bring it to any good, there must bee continuall labour bestowed thereon, by bringing into it good store of chalke, lime, or sand, or else ashes eyther of wood or of sea-coals.

—JOHN PARKINSON, *A Garden of Pleasant Flowers*

Modern gardeners might have some difficulty finding sea-coal, so the recommended method for today's gardeners is to use sand and compost. Sand is a permanent cure, but it can only be added a little at a time if it is to mix properly with the clay. Adding too much sand at any one time only creates the interesting problem of having a clay soil with sandy sections inside it. If you double dig, spreading ¼ to ½ inch of sand equally over the area to be dug before starting, this will be sufficient for one year. Every year the garden is dug, another quarter inch of sand can be spread and incorporated. It will take several years to see a large difference in the soil texture when using small amounts of sand. However, the sand will incorporate during the digging and the soil structure will permanently change to the depth of the digging. This process takes time, but it does work.

Temporary and faster-acting change can be had by adding large amounts of compost. Peter Henderson's recommendation of four and a half pounds of compost to the square foot would be sufficient to start a change during the first year of growing (Henderson [1866] 1895). The compost acts quickly when dug into the soil but is consumed in the process of decomposition. It must be replaced on a yearly basis if the soil is to improve. Easily available peat moss will work in the same way to separate the soil particles, though it will have no nutritional value until it begins to rot down, shedding its waxy coating.

A better solution is to combine the two, adding compost and sand on a yearly basis to continually adjust and enjoy the benefits of good soil.

WHEN THE SOIL is of a very heavy retentive clay, it should all be removed from the bed to a depth of 3 feet. The bottom should be sloped away from the direction where percolating water would enter it, giving a fall of about 1 inch in 2 feet . . . and then agricultural drain pipes should be laid to take the water right away.

—H. DRYSDALE WOODCOCK, K.C.; AND J. COUTTS, V.M.H., *Lilies: Their Culture and Management*

The ultimate solution is one of removal and drainage. However, removing a section from heavy clay and filling it in with good soil without drainage tile creates a form of in-ground flower pot. The drainage within the new soil is good, but the surrounding clay prevents any water movement out of the hole. It is like growing plants in a bathtub. Several days of heavy rain will create an overflow or bog garden instead of a garden bed. In order to remove the water from the hole, the bottom of the growing hole must be sloped toward a drainage tile that will transport the water away from the growing area. The slope will help the trapped water move toward the drainpipe and the drainpipe will move the water away. In this way, plants that require excellent drainage can be grown within pockets of clay. Digging holes in heavy clay soils and replacing the clay with good topsoil *without the use of drain pipes* is for gamblers. You will win a few extra blossoms during summers when the rains are favorable and you will lose the plants during those few summers when the rain is heavy. While our own gardens do not suffer from heavy clay, the one thing I have definitely learned in my years of gardening is that if I have to solve a problem, I only want to solve it once and I want to solve it the best way possible.

Gardens with clay soils benefit from general tile drainage. The tiles help move the water away from the soil in the spring, allowing the gardener to work the ground much earlier without the risk of creating clay chunks. Setting in good drainage tiles is a job for a landscape crew or someone who knows about surveying and land leveling lasers. It can be done by a homeowner with a strong back or access to digging equipment, a commitment to detail, and a willingness to follow a few simple rules. (Water runs downhill!) Check with your local extension office for information on farm drainage tiles; it's the same process.

Frances Perry, a respected English garden writer, noted in *The Woman Gardener* (1955) that clay soils would become more friable (a gardening word for good or workable) with the addition of lime, "if lime is spread on the ground however, it possesses the power in its breakdown to cause these fragments to 'dot' together, or become what is called 'flocculated'. By reason of such grouping, air spaces automatically form and we get better drainage and aeration." Howard Crane, in his book *Gardening on Clay* (1963), recommends eight ounces per square yard of lime to create this effect. Gardeners with clay soils and without the burning desire to install drainage pipes can experiment with adding the required eight ounces per square yard of lime and applying four pounds of compost per square foot as mentioned above, and seeing how this works on their particular soil. If it does not work, the only solutions are drainage tiles or growing plants that like clay conditions. Complaining to other gardeners about your heavy clay soil is good for the soul but has no immediate effect on the garden itself.

THEREFORE IF YOUR GROUND BE STIFF, trench with ferns, straw, bean-ham, thatch, litter earth under wood-stacks, small sticks &c. If gravelly or sandy, then trench and mix with loam or the upper part of clay; the turf of both is good.

—JOHN REID, *The Scots Gard'ner*

Too Much Sand

A garden with soil that is sandy has the opposite problem of that with too much clay. The water disappears too quickly and fertility levels are harder to maintain. Adding organic matter is a sound gardening principle as a first step. Organic matter acts to hold water and, as it breaks down into humus, it increases the fertility level of the soil. The trenching that John Reid (1907) refers to is the double digging mentioned earlier; even in 1638, digging was a fact of gardening life.

One trick as old as gardening is the use of turf as a soil additive. Many of the oldest English gardening books advise stacking the sod removed from the garden digging and allowing the pile to rot and compost for a year or two. The resulting composted soil is among the best of topsoils and will benefit any garden. Victorian gardeners thought so highly of this rotted turf they used it as potting soil in their greenhouses. Sod can be stacked, grass side down, in piles as tall as four feet and as wide as you have room for. If allowed to settle and overwinter, this will become excellent topsoil. There will be a layer of grass on the top of the pile; dig this off and turn it over to form the next pile. The good soil is below this green layer. This is wonderful when creating a new garden, but digging up the lawn or purchasing sod is an expensive way to obtain topsoil. Sometimes garden centers have old sod that has dried out and died, or is being discarded because it remains unsold at the end of the season; piling this material will create excellent topsoil.

THE LOVE OF DIRT is among the earliest of passions, as it is the latest. Mud pies gratify one of our first and best instincts. So long as we are dirty, we are pure. Fondness for the ground comes back to a man after he has run the round of pleasure and business, eaten dirt, and sown wild-oats, drifted about the world, and taken the wind of all its moods. The love of digging in the ground (or of looking on while he pays another to dig) is as sure to come back to him as he is sure, at last to go under the ground and stay there. To own a bit of ground, to scratch it with a hoe, to plant seeds, and watch their renewal of life — this is . . . the most satisfactory thing a man can do.

— CHARLES DUDLEY WARNER, *My Summer in a Garden*

Another method for improving sandy soils is to purchase bentonite clay particles and slowly add them to your garden soils. Bentonite clay is usually available through well-drilling companies if not at your neighborhood garden center. Add this in ¼-inch increments per year over the garden bed (similar to the addition of sand to clay soils) to slowly increase the clay component of sandy soils. Spread and work the dry clay into the soil immediately without allowing the clay to become wet; damp bentonite is a sticky mess. Keep the bag in a dry location; it is a truly amazing sight to watch a bag of this material swell and turn into a greasy mound when it absorbs water. If a choice has to be made between the clay and compost, choose the compost, but if both can be worked into sandy soils, then real soil will slowly start to appear.

Another solution adopted by some gardeners is to purchase proper topsoil, mixing it into the sandy soil. This method does come with a warning about establishing the quality of the topsoil before purchasing it. Bagged topsoils are often heavily laced with manures and peat moss to give them the dark appearance so important for visual appeal and instant, if short-lived, garden success. They are much more expensive than simply purchasing the peat and manure separately. In our neighborhood, the topsoil is quite sandy so any truckloads being purchased to repair sandy soils will only be slightly better than the existing soil. If the sandy soil is modern suburban sand backfill, then purchasing topsoil is a good step. If the soil is merely sandy, then adding organic matter is the cheapest and most effective, if never-ending, solution. Your soil will be the better for it.

Regardless of whether your garden is four acres wide or just four thousand miles deep, the soil is (excuse the pun) at the bottom of it. At the bottom does not, as should be clear by now, mean at the lowest gardening priority but rather that it is the basis for success or failure. And whether the gardener sees working the soil as a romantic event, an exercise and stress work-out, or just a let's-get-it-done activity, the soil still has to receive its due attention if the garden is to succeed.

Our gardening ancestors had the right emphasis. How indeed can we do otherwise?

Next to position, soil is the most important element in the formation of a garden. In selecting a soil, two things should be kept in view — first, that an open or well-drained soil assists climate (that is, the more porous a soil is the warmer is the ground, and the better able to withstand extreme cold are the plants); and secondly, that the soil should be deep.

— Robinson, *The English Flower Garden*

CHAPTER TWO

PERENNIALS

LENTE SUSCIPE CITO PERFICE

Set out at leisure, proceed with haste.

—A BOOK OF SUNDIAL MOTTOES

ere this a book of true confessions rather than a book on gardening, this is where I would have to bare my soul. I grow more perennials than any gardener really needs and every year I feed the addiction by adding to my collection. Fortunately, this is not a confessional and I am spared the need to wax poetic about each and every plant in the garden. I suspect this is likely lucky for us both. Designing a perennial garden is one of those wonderful gardening activities that is never truly finished, or totally "right." There is always room for improvement. Beginners sometimes make the mistake of thinking of a perennial garden as just a longer-lived annual garden: Install it and then let it grow.

IF I WERE TO MAKE a garden, another garden, a new garden, I should probably make mistakes as I have done in the past, mistakes like every reader of this has made and will make. There is no royal road or clean-cut path to the making of a garden.

—E. H. WILSON, *If I Were to Make a Garden*

A perennial garden is a hands-on garden. Its success or failure depends on the amount of time spent with it. Maintenance

NAMING PERENNIALS

The plaintive call of the beginning gardener is a common sound of spring in the perennial nursery business. It sounds something like "Why can't they use *real* names on these plants?" They are complaining about the horticultural use of the Latin binomial, or two-name system of identifying plants. Each plant has a Latin name as a unique identifier, just as you have a name that identifies you. Gardeners all over the world discuss individual plants and keeping them straight demands a scientific rigidity. For example, bellflower is a beautiful name for at least three plant families that have bell-like flowers. (Campanula is only one of them and there are at least two hundred species of campanula.) If we called them all bellflowers, we would never sort out what we were talking about. Gardeners use horticultural Latin so that each plant will have a unique name shared by no other plant on the planet. When we call a plant by its Latin name, everybody knows exactly which one we are discussing.

As NEW AND STRANGE PLANTS were brought by curious-minded people into gardens, a real difficulty in the matter of providing them with names arose. Many of us today are amused at the seriousness the botanist attaches to mere names. Sometimes we

is one of the aspects of perennial gardening so easily glossed over by garden center salespeople. It takes much more maintenance to have a good perennial garden than it ever does to have an annual garden of the same size. To be sure, the perennials wish most devoutly that he coin less tongue-twisting names, but what we suffer at his hands is as nothing compared to what the would-be student of plants in the early eighteenth century endured. For example, *Acer Americanum, folia majore, suptus argenteo, supre viridi splendente, floribus multis coccineus* is the way Miller in his first edition of his Dictionary set forth our common Red Maple, which Linnaeus later dubbed *Acer rubrum.*

—E. H. WILSON, *If I Were to Make a Garden*

Are you alone in your distaste for the Latin binomial system? Likely not. One of the greatest names in English horticulture, William Robinson (1905), wrote, "English names are given where possible—as it is best to speak of things growing about our doors in our own tongue, and the practice of using in conversation long Latin names, a growth of our own century, has done infinite harm to gardening in shutting out people who have a heart for a garden, but none for the Latin of the gardener."

However, when you order a *Campanula carpatica* 'Blue Clips' you know exactly what you will get for your garden. If you ordered a bellflower, you never know just what might arrive in the mail.

HAREBELL

come back from year to year—at least we hope they do—thereby saving the yearly cost of replanting. But that cost is more than made up by the need to do all labor by hand, to constantly deadhead and prune, to divide and dig plants to keep them healthy and thriving. Annual gardening is decorating; perennial gardening is truly gardening.

THE FAVOURITE PLAN of the average jobbing gardener who undertakes to lay out a new garden is to surround it on all sides with Privet hedges, and plant clumps of common Laurel, *Aucuba japonica*, common Thuya or Cupresus, to "afford shelter" as they say. It is sadly uneducated taste that finds enjoyment in the daily contemplation of these dull features of the usual run of suburban gardens.

— A. J. MacSelf, *Hardy Perennials*

And gardening is the delight of my life. It is never finished; as I change my gardening point of view, I vary the plants in the garden. As I find plants I would like to grow, that attract my sense of color or adventure, I replace the older plants with the new. As my trees mature, the shade they throw changes the nature of the plants around our front yard—I am moving away from roses to hostas, trilliums, arisaemas, pulmonaria, and other shade-loving delights. The garden changes to reflect the gardener and his or her environment and this, too, is gardening rather than decorating.

While this book will not deal with design, one aspect of planning a perennial garden that garden centers and beginning designers often miss is how many plants it takes to fill up a garden. Many perennials expand over the years to capture more and more garden territory and it is always difficult to know exactly where to begin.

But for all practical intents and purposes, every 6 inches of ground could contain its plant, so that no 6 inches of bare ground need obtrude on the eye. Almost any kind of bare rock has a certain beauty, but I cannot say bare ground is ever beautiful.

— Frank Miles, as quoted in *The English Flower Garden*

We have found — on average — the initial design should contain one plant for every one-and-a-half square feet of garden space. Some of the small plants such as monarda will turn into garden monsters while others such as aquilegia will quietly hold their own but not expand the mother plant much beyond three-fourths of a square foot. If the gardener sticks to this number, the planning will come out right, and the garden will fill in within two to three years depending on soil and water conditions. Thicker planting — every plant being given one square foot — will fill the garden faster but will require much earlier renovation. In this I disagree with Mr. Miles when he recommends that plants be installed every six inches. In my experience, six inches is too close a planting unless we are talking about specialist alpine plants. Thinner planting will delay the need for renovation but will leave too many spaces that will have to be filled with annuals.

But for the busy or inexperienced plant-lover, where little care and attention can be given their culture, or where they are depended upon entirely to beautify the garden or to produce a supply of cut flowers, annuals and biennials have often proved to be only a source of disappointment and failure.

—Linus Woolverton, ed., *The Canadian Horticulturalist*

Filling the garden spaces with hardy annuals is a grand tradition in perennial gardening and one that should be encouraged in the initial stages of the newly planted perennial border.

Digging

Digging is one of those garden activities you love to hate. I will not try to convince the reader that digging is good for you or that it will make you younger and more attractive to the opposite sex. While these things are undoubtedly true, all I know is that my garden works better and the plants are stronger when I dig it and treat it properly than when I ignore it. There is a garden tip that I should pass along about digging that will make this task more agreeable. It is unbelievably simple.

The time for digging should always be chosen, if possible, when the ground is tolerably dry; not only on account of the danger of taking cold by standing on the damp earth, but because the soil, when damp, adheres to the spade, and is much more difficult to work (as the gardeners call it) than when it is dry.

—Jane Loudon, *Gardening for Ladies and Companion to the Flower Garden*

Use a sharp shovel. Many garden shovels never see a sharpening file or grindstone from one end of their life to the other. This is unfortunate, because a sharp shovel does more work with

less effort, and a few minutes spent filing and maintaining an edge will more than pay for themselves in the reduced stress on your back and legs.

As few ladies are strong enough to throw the earth from the heap where it was laid from the first furrow to fill the last, the best way is to put it into a small wheel-barrow, which may be wheeled to the place required, and filled and emptied as often as may be found convenient; or the ground may be divided into narrower strips.

—Jane Loudon, *Gardening for Ladies and Companion to the Flower Garden*

LADY'S WHEELBARROW

Let me just add that Mrs. Loudon lived in a different age than mine and her opinion about the strength of ladies and their ability to wield a shovel differs from my experience with three daughters and numerous female friends who have much larger or better gardens than my own. Let us leave it at that and move along to safer ground.

Planting

The first step in perennial gardening is putting plants into the ground and this certainly does not sound like a difficult task to master. Dig a hole, pop in the plant to the same level it was in the pot, backfill, soak with water to ensure good root contact with the soil, toss a few handfuls of compost around the plant, and sit back to enjoy its growth. In the majority of cases, this is really all it takes, so beginning gardeners need not worry themselves over the mastery of the task. My experience is that plants really know what they are about and that given half a chance they will grow quite nicely when provided with good soil, water, and the correct amount of sunshine.

IT IS INDEED astonishing that the asters, helianthus, rudbeckias, silphiums, and numberless other fine North American plants, all so easily grown and so handsome, should be entirely neglected in English gardens, and this in favour of carpets, hearthrugs, and ribbons, forming patterns of violent colours, which, though admired for being the fashion on the lawn and borders of our gardens and grounds, would not be tolerated on the floor of a drawing-room or boudoir.

—WILLIAM ROBINSON, *The English Flower Garden*

Knowing what plant to put in your garden or which plant will survive your climate is certainly another matter. We can, with some ease, give hints about the hardiness of plants in the garden. It is my gardening experience that a large number of plant tags and garden catalogs suggesting hardiness zones are, if not completely wrong, at least contradictory to one another. Plants that thrive in my Zone 4 garden are sometimes described as requiring a much warmer Zone 6 garden, and other plants that, according to the experts, anyone can grow in Zone 4 never survive a single winter season for me. Garden soil conditions and siting are much more impor-

RUDBECKIA

tant than slavishly following a zone chart. For example, I have a large lavender collection while nearby gardeners despair of ever growing this plant. The difference is that I grow mine in a very sandy soil while their plants are grown in clay. If you remember no other tip from this book, remember this one. The majority of perennial plants do not like clay soils—winter survival rates will be dramatically lowered by heavier clay soils than by any other reason. Consider this every time you plant a new perennial.

As we have often had occasion to observe, the proper application of the word "hardy" is a source of great difficulty to the horticultural writer, as the hardiness of a plant is regulated by so many circumstances other than mere temperature.

    —EDWARD SPRAGUE RAND, JR., *Bulbs: A Treatise on Hardy and Tender Bulbs and Tubers*

It is very evident from all this, we think, that we cannot form any decisive opinion as to what is and what is not truly hardy in any one portion of the country, where we receive so many contradictory reports; but it does not follow that a failure for one or two years, unless very complete, should discourage us so entirely as to prevent our trying the same plant again in other situations and under different treatment.

    —HENRY SARGENT, SUPPLEMENT TO THE SIXTH EDITION OF *Landscape Gardening*

I also note that siting within the garden is critical for success. Tender plants tucked up next to large rocks in my alpine garden grow much better than when asked to grow in a more exposed condition. The rocks absorb the heat from the sun, bringing the critical small temperature difference between surviving and becoming compost to the rest of the garden. My tender shrubs, when planted in the lee of the house and out of drying winter winds grow well; especially if we compare them to the dead stalks left standing in the more open pond gardens a hundred yards away.

The other factor in garden planting that I confess my bias toward is growing good plants. I remember the horror of a visitor when we were taking a tour of my garden and we came across an aquilegia blooming for the first time. It was a horrid shade of muddy pink and did neither itself nor my garden proud, so I yanked it out on the spot. My friend was aghast, but I certainly did not want this ugly plant to self-sow in my garden, and I had much more delightful aquilegia elsewhere. "Get rid of the beast," I said. There are too many good plants available in nurseries and catalogs to spend limited garden space and time on poor examples. I was delighted a few years later to read William Robinson and find he agreed with me – or, more humbly, I agreed with him. How could I go wrong following the advice

WILD COLUMBINE

of this great writer: "Select only good plants; throw away weedy kinds, there is no scarcity of the best" (Robinson 1905). If this was true in the nineteenth century when first written, it is certainly true today.

BLOOM TIMES

One of the delightful features of perennial plants is that they only bloom for a short period of time. I know this is contrary to what most gardeners want—a long bloom time—but with my short attention span, I can have a different color theme in all three major gardening seasons in my perennial gardens. My spring garden tends to softer colors with a lot of pinks and blues. The summer garden starts to heat up with more and more reds showing up while the fall garden shouts its gardening good-byes with its yellows and hot reds. How boring it would be if I only had one color to last me all summer!

THE MAIN CHARM of bedding plants—that of lasting in bloom a long time— is really a drawback. It is the stereotyped kind of garden which we have to fight against; we want beautiful and changeful gardens, and should therefore have the flowers of each season. Too short a bloom is a misfortune; but so is too long a bloom, and numbers of hardy plants bloom quite as long as can be desired.

—WILLIAM ROBINSON, *The English Flower Garden*

When designing my perennial flower gardens, I assume four to six weeks of bloom for most of my plants. To be sure, there are a few that bloom slightly longer, and some even shorter, but for the most part, four to six weeks does the trick with the design.

FEEDING

In my own perennial gardens, I feed much more lightly than in the vegetable garden. Vegetables, roses, and water garden plants get a full measure of food, but I find perennials do better with less. This is not to suggest I starve the perennials but rather that I do not overfeed them, creating a lush, rampant growth that requires staking and a dedication to pruning that is not healthy for either my body or spirit. In many cases, delphiniums for example, I try to avoid feeding at all if possible. Overfed delphiniums tend to fall over in the slightest wind and require staking if they are to be seen as anything more than a flower stalk drooped over a nearby rose. Lush, nitrogen-rich delphiniums also tend to die over the winter much more readily than their somewhat shorter, hardier, and undeniably hungrier cousins. I find ½ inch of compost spread over the perennial beds in the very early spring or late fall sees to all the perennial plant feeding needs. Our perennial beds also benefit from a thick mulch, the bottom layers of which are constantly decomposing and providing organic matter to feed the garden. I do not liquid feed the perennials at all during the summer, unlike the roses that thrive on a weekly dose of fish emulsion or manure tea.

IT HAS BEEN FOUND, from experience, that plants imbibe more food than they absolutely require as nourishment from the soil, and that they eject part of it;

also that their roots will not re-imbibe this excrementious matter, but are continually in search of fresh soil.

— JANE LOUDON, *Gardening for Ladies and Companion to the Flower Garden*

Mrs. Loudon seems to think that plants eject part of their plant food and will not take it up again. While I dare not speak to the molecular biology of such a concept, I rather doubt that this has much practical merit from a gardener's point of view. Plants are not "continually in search of fresh soil" in the sense that the only way to have a good garden is to replace the soil. They are in search of nutrition and grow better if we provide it by regular applications of compost or ample organic matter that will degrade into humus in the garden.

PROPAGATING PERENNIALS

One of the delights of real gardening is propagating your own plants, whether by cuttings, seed, or divisions. Mastering these basic techniques will enable the gardener to expand the range of plants in the garden. Often the more unusual plants are passed along over the back fence or through horticultural societies; understanding the basics of plant propagation is the first step in receiving and successfully growing the shared garden bounty.

Propagating from Cuttings

SOMETIMES, THE POTS are sunk into a hotbed, to induce the cuttings to take root, and this is called applying bottom heat; and sometimes one flower-pot is placed within another a size or two larger, and the inner one filled with

1. BADLY TRIMMED, THE CUT
BEING TOO FAR BELOW JOINT.

2. CORRECT SQUARE CUT
AT BASE OF JOINT.

3. CUTTING WITH NEATLY
TRIMMED "HEEL."

SUITABLE SHOOTS FOR CUTTINGS

water (the hole at the bottom being first stopped with clay or putty), and the cuttings placed in the outer one.

—JANE LOUDON, *Gardening for Ladies and Companion to the Flower Garden*

JUST WHY OR HOW this mysterious change takes place in the cell structure, enabling the plant to develop a root system at a point which normally would have remained but a piece of smooth stem, far above the ground, we do not know.

—FREDERICK ROCKWELL, *Gardening with Peat Moss*

I find that the vast majority of perennials root easily from cuttings taken from the growing tips of the plant. While I have rooted quarter-inch-long cuttings of *Phlox subulata*, I like to keep the cuttings a bit longer—say two to three inches in length—to reduce the stress on the plant.

SOMETIMES THE GROWTH is so short or the stock so scarce that the cutting cannot be made long enough to hold itself in the soil. In such case, a toothpick or splinter is tied to the cutting to hold it erect.

—LIBERTY HYDE BAILEY, *The Nursery Book*

At my cutting bench, I also use an antidesiccant—sometimes sold as Christmas tree preservative—which is sprayed on the leaves to stop them from losing moisture. With the antidesiccant, the leaves do not wilt and therefore root much easier. To make sure the cutting has enough moisture available for good root development, I use the pot-in-pot system and I put the pots in a white plastic bag to further reduce moisture loss. The bag is opened up daily to reduce the excess moisture, but the white plastic reduces the stress level on the cutting. I have also used a glass cloche over the top of a single flowerpot to accomplish the same thing. More modern gardeners could cut the bottom off a large plastic soda bottle to create a mini-greenhouse. If either the glass cloche or soda bottle is

POT-IN-POT PROPAGATION

used, the cuttings should be kept in the shade during the rooting process. These clear containers can easily generate a heat that is high enough to kill the cuttings. There is no question that bottom heat, keeping the soil temperature to 72°F, encourages the cutting to root quickly.

Bottom heat is always essential to the best success with cuttings.
—Liberty Hyde Bailey, *The Nursery Book*

Being from a colder climate, I use a readily available roof de-icer cable controlled with a horticultural thermostat (available through mail-order catalogs) to maintain an even soil temperature. Thermostat-controlled bottom heating mats also work well and these, too, are available through the mail. I set my pot-in-pot systems directly on the heating cable or mat and this very quickly brings the soil to the correct rooting temperature.

SOFT CUTTINGS ARE commonly cut below a bud or cut to a heel, but this is unnecessary in easily rooted plants like geranium, coleus, heliotrope, etc.

— LIBERTY HYDE BAILEY, *The Nursery Book*

Propagating by Seed

LET NO ONE THINK that real gardening is a bucolic and meditative occupation. It is an insatiable passion, like everything else to which a man gives his heart.

— KAREL CAPEK, *The Gardener's Year*

I confess to being a confirmed seedaholic. An incurable case, I am afraid, and while I will not bore you with the details of this condition, let me assure you while it is an extremely virulent disease it poses no long-term, serious health risk. Those who develop a full-blown case are generally found poring over catalogs and collector seed lists, muttering incantations over flowerpots, and transplanting hundreds of tiny green plants into garden receptacles of all manner and shape. These people are harmless but happy in their own right.

WATER IS NECESSARY for seeds to induce them to germinate; but much of it is very injurious to young plants when they first come up, as it unsettles their roots, and almost washes them away. The roots, also, are at first too weak to imbibe water; and the plants feed on the nourishment contained in the cotyledons, or in the albumen of the seeds.

— JANE LOUDON, *Gardening for Ladies and Companion to the Flower Garden*

Seed lovers generally follow several different methods for germinating their future loves. All methods use a sterilized or pasteurized soil or artificial soil medium, so let me start by suggesting that boiling water is the easiest way to sterilize garden soil or potting soil that I know. If a pot is filled with soil and boiling water is very slowly poured in until the liquid is freely running out the bottom, it will kill the vast majority of soilborne weeds or pathogens. This works equally well on bagged potting soil or plunged pots out in the garden. ("Plunging" is one of those gardening words and it simply means to bury the pot up to its rim in the soil.)

Perennial seeds germinate according to their internal hormonal rhythms, and it is a gardener's task in life to decipher these rhythms. The following are some of the more common methods used by confirmed seedaholics. A regular flowerpot filled with sterilized soil is the most basic tool of our seed trade. The soil is tamped down lightly, the seed is distributed over the top, and then the all-important covering is added. Few of the elite in the seed germination fraternity use soil to cover their seed. Instead, they use chick grit or turface. Chick grit, available from country agricultural stores or bird-feeding stores, provides a good covering because it is heavy and not likely to be washed away by a splurt of water. It also retards the growth of algae and lichens that are prone to appear on pots that are left for any length of time awaiting seed germination. Turface, often available through larger garden suppliers or furnace oil dealers (they use it as an oil spill absorber) is a claylike product that acts in

much the same way as chick grit. Turface and chick grit are inter-
changeable if used as a seed covering.

IT IS A GENERAL RULE, *in transplanting, never to bury the collar of a plant.*
— JANE LOUDON, *Gardening for Ladies and Companion to the Flower Garden*

Sometimes turface is used all by itself, with no soil, to germinate extremely small or delicate seeds. Fill a small pot with
turface, sprinkle the seed over the surface (don't cover very
fine seed), and then set the pot in a small bowl of
water. The turface will soak up the water to provide exactly the correct level of moisture needed
by the germinating seeds. Keep the bowl of water
filled until the seeds germinate. Do not water the
turface from the top, as this will wash the tiny
seedlings down into the crevices.

Those gardeners with spare drawer space
in their refrigerator may want to try the Baggie
method of seed germination. Many perennial
seeds require a dormancy period and a refrigerator
is the perfect spot to provide this faux-winter. Put a
tablespoon of slightly damp vermiculite — vermiculite is available at most garden centers — into the
Baggie. Put the seed into the vermiculite and seal
the bag. Put this bag in the crisper of the refrigerator — not the freezer — for ninety days. Take it out and
sow the seed as above. Germination of most perennial seeds takes place quite quickly after sowing.

EVENING
PRIMROSE

Naturally, there are some weeds that take their time germinating over the next ninety days, some that demand another ninety-day cold treatment (called double dormancy) after the ninety days of warmth, and some that simply refuse to grow. We normally call the latter "dead."

Let us bear in mind that however favoured and well appointed a garden may be, there will be some plants that refuse to thrive, baffling sometimes even the utmost care of expert cultivators.

—A. J. MacSelf, *The Hardy Perennials*

Far and away the easiest system of germinating perennial seeds is to use the outdoor method. The easiest system is to plunge the sown pot into a protected spot in the garden where it can be watered and easily cared for. Leave the seeds out summer and winter until they germinate. Unless the seed is a notorious slow germinator such as trillium, dig up the pots and empty them after the third unsuccessful spring. Once the seeds germinate in their pots, dig up the pots and transplant the seedlings into their own pots for growing on until they are large enough to go directly into the garden. A variation on this is to cut the bottom off a small nursery pot (the flexible plastic type) and plunge the bottomless pot into the garden soil. Sterilize the garden soil by soaking the area with boiling water. The soil will be left in place when the pot is shoved into the soil—then sow the seeds inside the pot. This is as natural a seeding environment as is possible to provide, and the resulting seedlings are treated as any others. This is an excellent system for forgetful gardeners because it demands the least amount of attention.

Propagating by Division

THE WORD DIVISION is commonly applied to that phase of separation in which the parts are cut or broken into pieces, in distinction to propagation by means of parts which naturally separate at the close of the season; but no hard and fast line can be drawn between the two operations.

— LIBERTY HYDE BAILEY, *The Nursery Book*

Although some gardeners promote differing methods of dividing perennials, I have found two rules of thumb that work well for me. The first concerns timing. *If it blooms in the spring, divide it in the fall. If it blooms in the fall, divide it in the spring.* This little proverb has worked well for me for the past twenty-five years, and the only question I ever get is when to divide the summer bloomers. The honest answer is that I do it whenever I have the time, spring or fall; it does not seem to matter. In our cold Zone 4 garden, I do ensure that all perennial work is finished by the end of September. I have found over the years that planting and dividing after this date reduces the chances of success and increases the amount of winter-kill on the plants. Gardeners in warmer zones can add a week of work time into October for every zone warmer than Zone 4.

IF THE WEATHER is hot and bright, a few sheets of newspaper placed over the newly transplanted plants, and held in position by small stones or a few handfuls of earth, will help to maintain a more humid atmosphere around the plant.

— FREDERICK ROCKWELL, *Gardening with Peat Moss*

Despite Mr. Rockwell's advice about covering plants, I do not think this is necessary in the fall. The plants are entering dormancy and the division thrusts them, rather rudely I suppose, into full dormancy. However, if you transplant in summer, contrary to much modern convention that says you should not attempt it, use this newspaper trick to good advantage. Do keep the soil quite damp on summer transplants for the first few weeks to reduce stress on the plants as much as possible. You can move perennials in the midst of the summer, particularly if you take as much soil with the plant as possible and do not disturb the roots. It is, however, not common practice and not recommended if you can avoid it.

PLANTS . . . MAY now be readily transplanted with small balls of earth about their roots, it should be done accordingly, and the plants will thus scarcely feel any check by removal; or let others be removed with as full roots as possible, planting the whole, in the allotted places, in a varied order; and give directly an immediate watering to settle the earth closely about the roots.

— THOMAS MAWE AND JOHN ABERCROMBIE, *The Complete Gardener*

The second rule of thumb I follow is to ignore much of the accepted modern wisdom about dividing perennials. I see many recent books recommending the use of two garden forks, back-to-back, to pry roots apart and providing various arcane directions for dividing perennials. As for me, using a sharpened shovel, I simply whack off a chunk that looks big enough to thrive. As long as the perennial piece has at least one or two old stalks up top and a web of roots on the bottom, it will thrive nicely in its new spot. If, with plants such as dianthus or lavender, I cannot find a way to get old top growth and good roots, I propagate them from cuttings or seed. Those single-stalked perennials are not good candidates for dividing.

THE USE OF WATERING a transplanted plant, is as obvious as that of shading. It is simply to supply the spongioles with an abundance of food, that the increased quantity imbibed by each, may, in some degree, supply their diminished number.

—JANE LOUDON, *Gardening for Ladies and Companion to the Flower Garden*

MAINTENANCE

There is little doubt that the true test of a gardener is found not in the rare plants he or she grows, nor in the garden design, but rather in the overall maintenance of the garden. A well-maintained yet simple garden is to be preferred to any dazzlingly weedy display of plant treasures. I tell myself this constantly as I do my own weeding. I confess I have had both treasures and weeds in my time as a gardener, and the weed-free garden is much more enjoyable. It

WILD GERANIUM

is truly difficult to see the artistry in a garden when one has to confront pigweed, dandelions, and mustard, all plants not likely part of the initial planting scheme.

WE HOLD THAT the only true test of our efforts in planting or gardening is the picture. Do we frighten the artist away, or do we bring him to see a garden so free from ugly patterns and ugly colours that, seen in a beautiful light, it would be worth painting? There is not, and there never can be, any other true test.

— WILLIAM ROBINSON, *The English Flower Garden*

I use more mulch than any other gardener I know. All of my garden beds are mulched, the flowers with bark chips, the vegetables with straw, and the alpine beds with pea-gravel. The mulch does delay my spring garden by keeping the soil cooler for longer into the spring, but this is more than made up for by its ability to retard the growth of weeds in my garden. My thick layer of mulch means I can enjoy my garden without constantly having a weeding tool in my hands. The mulch does several other things for the perennial gardens. It preserves a constant supply of moisture and keeps the soil temperatures cool enough for the plants during our high heat days of July and early August. As it rots down, it provides extra organic matter to the soil. (See the previous discussion of soil organic matter.) As a final note, it provides a food source for earwigs. Earwigs prefer to eat rotting organic matter over almost all other food. If I give them mulch to eat, they do not wander up to live on or eat my flower blossoms. I confess it is a trade off—the earwigs get to live and I get my flower blossoms. This is a simple solution but an elegant and happy one for all concerned. This mulch may be a problem in areas such as the northwest United States because of the moist conditions and the slugs that result. While I do not have much slug damage because the slugs tend to stay below the mulch as well, in places with more rainfall and less severe winters, the mulch might contribute to the problem rather than being a solution.

I NOTE, FOR EXAMPLE, that lawn-mowings are not wasted. They are spread in a thin mulch over beds. Thin, because if you heap them too thickly they heat; therefore, never spread them more than two or three inches deep. The virtue of lawn-mowings is threefold: they keep the weeds away, they retain moisture, and they supply humus to the soil as the green stuff rots down and returns its vegetable value into the ground it grew from.

— VITA SACKVILLE-WEST, *More for Your Garden*

A new product arriving on the market as an organic weed preventative is corn gluten. This byproduct of corn milling is eaten by humans as well as animals, yet it has the curious ability to stop small seeds from germinating when spread over the soil. If applied to lawns and gardens at twenty pounds of corn gluten to a thousand square feet of ground, it will stop seeds such as dandelion and crabgrass from germinating. To be effective it *has* to be applied before these target seeds have germinated; this normally means applying the gluten while the forsythia are in bloom. If applied after the weed seeds have germinated, it will have no effect on them. It will not stop larger seeds such as corn

or beans from germinating nor will it affect established plants.
It is available in the organic remedies section at environment-
friendly garden centers and in feed mills.

Mawe and Abercrombie wrote a wonderful description of
how to clean and maintain the perennial border and even after
150 years, it contains the essential duties of the perennial gardener. They write for April tasks,

> First destroy weeds in every part before they grow large;
> they will now rise numerously in the borders &c.
>
> Let these be destroyed by the hoe or hand, as it is most
> convenient; but where the plants stand wide, let the hoe be
> used, it being the most expeditious method.
>
> Let the hoe be sharp; take advantage of a dry day to use
> it, cutting the weeds up clean within the surface; and let
> every part between the plants be stirred; and as you go on,
> let all dead leaves and straggling shoots be taken off.
>
> Then rake the borders, &c., over neatly with a small
> rake; clearing away, at the same time, all the weeds and
> litter, and let the surface be made perfectly clean and
> smooth; and they will thus have a requisite, fresh, orderly
> appearance, agreeably for the spring season (Mawe and
> Abercrombie n.d.).

He is right: Get the weeds and get them early, use sharp
tools, and leave the garden looking good. What else could a
modern writer possibly add?

RENOVATION

It is a curious fact that garden centers seldom talk to their customers about perennial garden renovation. In accounting for my gardening time, I would have to say that I spend more time renovating and maintaining the perennial plants than on any other part of my gardens. The alpine gardens are the most labor intensive, followed by the main perennial borders. In planting, we somehow seem to forget that perennial plants keep expanding. That the monarda and macleaya will, if planted together, fraternize and try to outcolonize the other. We forget that the wonderful *Lysimachia clethroides* we planted for cut flowers is nothing short of a garden thug—resembling Attila the Hun more than a gentle flower for the cutting garden. Perennial plants require garden work and this is both their strength and their weakness. Is it any wonder that Vita Sackville-West (1955) wrote, "In the old days when many gardeners were employed, staking and weeding, it probably made a good effect. No so today. 'Dig it all up,' we said. 'Scrap it. Simplify. Make a broad green walk, quiet and austere, to be mown once a week. And on no account smother the walls with climbers. Whatever there is must be special and choice. Simplify.'"

Simplify indeed. I wish it were that simple. I think it may be and then I see the perfect plant for that special garden spot and very shortly, I am back to having to control

ASCLEPIAS TUBEROSA

and maintain my garden because the plant population is once again growing and expanding.

There are two main systems of perennial border control. The first is the ongoing maintenance system. In this operation, plants are divided or edged back when they seem to require it. If a plant is not outgrowing its boundaries and presents no problem, leave it to its own devices. If a plant has no obviously large dead spots within its central core, it is not a candidate for digging and dividing off the new and vigorous shoots and replanting these while discarding the dead central core. Under the ongoing maintenance system, add compost each year and when a plant requires lifting and dividing, add extra compost— one or two shovelsful—to that area to give the newly divided plant a boost.

All the care these require is to keep them free from grass and weeds, giving them occasional top-dressing of well-rotted manure, and when they seem to have become overgrown or tired of their position, giving them a shift to a new spot, and, if need be, dividing the root.

—Delors W. Beadle, *Canadian Fruit, Flower, and Kitchen Gardener*

The second system is used once every decade or so when the entire border is starting to look a little overgrown or the gardener has decided it is time to overhaul the garden design. Sometimes, grass has invaded or the soil needs a complete redigging and revitalization. This is the everybody-out-of-the-garden time. Remove all plants from their spots, double dig the soil, compost well, and then reinstall the plants in the new design or arrangement. It is simply amazing how easily one can write this sentence and how much backbreaking work it takes to accomplish it.

A LARGE PIECE OF GROUND may soon be gone over with a hoe, when the weeds are small; but when they are permitted to grow large, it requires double labour to destroy them.

—THOMAS MAWE AND JOHN ABERCROMBIE, *The Complete Gardener*

LABELING PLANTS

One of the biggest debates in Internet gardening mailing lists is how to create a lasting label. If you are like me, your memory is good — but short, and the name of the plant that was installed a few years ago tends to fade right along with the label that came with it.

Do NOT PAY much attention to labelling; if a plant is not worth knowing, it is not worth growing; let each good thing be so bold and so well known as to make its presence felt.

—WILLIAM ROBINSON, *The English Flower Garden*

I also confess I do try to grow only the best plants, those that will make an impression on my mind. Robinson had it right, you know; if you

SPIDERWORT

grow the bold plant that makes "its presence felt," you will remember names without resorting to tags. However, bury the tag at the front of the plant to be sure.

In my garden, I plant the label right along with the plant. I sink the plastic label at the front of the plant so that at some time in the future if I really need to know the name, I can dig it up and identify it. Sunk in the ground, it does not fade and does not get fragile due to sunlight degradation. Oh, to be sure, I have always labeled the plants in the display gardens around our nursery. I find embossing tape to be the best choice and I stick and staple the tapes to a smooth wood stake so that I can read them from a few feet away. I do resent the resemblance to hundreds of grave markers that these stakes create when the flowers do not completely hide them. I am also experimenting with flat stones in the rock garden; I write the name of the plant on the stone and turn the stone upside down next to the plant.

CHAPTER THREE

ANNUALS

Noiseless falls the foot of time which only treads on flowers.

—A BOOK OF SUNDIAL MOTTOES

fter a long winter, who can resist the temptation of a yellow spring pansy or deep violet heliotrope? Who indeed can resist the pleasure of planting these alluring fragrant temptresses with their promises of summer delights? I know I seldom can. Gardeners fall for these charmers by the millions every spring and revel in their planting and care. Garden writers are no better able to resist and have been writing about annuals for years, putting them into one of three distinct categories. However, just to make life interesting, authors often disagree about which category a favorite plant occupies. Fortunately, most of this disagreement stems from the home geography of the author rather than from any plot to confuse beginning gardeners. What is a tender annual in California may very well become a half-hardy annual in New Hampshire.

Roy Biles in his classic *The Complete Book of Garden Magic* (1950) defines annual categories in this way:

> *Tender annuals.* These annuals may be sown outdoors after all danger of frost *or* may be sown indoors before frost to obtain a good head start on the growing season.
>
> *Half-hardy annuals.* These annuals require a long growing season before blooming. Because of this long development time, they are started in greenhouses or cold frames before being transplanted into the garden.
>
> *Hardy annuals.* These plants are best sown in the garden where they are to grow. These plants may resent transplanting or may simply grow too quickly for ease of starting and transplanting indoors.

In an attempt to simplify these definitions, some authors lump tender annuals and half-hardy annuals into the same category (Perry 1955). If the plant is started indoors, it is called a half-hardy plant, and if started outdoors, hardy. The rationale for this is that if a plant is tender enough that a light frost will damage it, it should be kept in a greenhouse until all danger is over. Plants that are at all tender will do better in a greenhouse and will flower more completely with a protected start. This is an easy method of sorting out annuals and I confess that, as a gardener, I much prefer the simpler system.

No gardener will wish to fill her garden with annuals, but for stop gaps while more permanent material is getting established, they are invaluable.

—Frances Perry, *The Woman Gardener*

It is also fair to point out that many gardeners believe that annual flowers are not worthy of being the sole flowering focal points in the garden. This negative attitude is widespread in the gardening world, but, as in all things, every person is responsible for his or her own gardening pleasure. If annuals fit the bill, why, then the bill is well paid with a full range of annual flowers in the garden.

Hardy Annuals

It is an inescapable fact that hardy annuals perform a yeoman's duty in the garden. There is no cheaper way of obtaining scads of blooms than to use hardy annuals sown directly into the garden. Gardeners who look down their noses at the annuals have lost contact with their history. John Parkinson ([1629] 1907) said it best: "To prescribe one forme for every man to follow, were too great presumption and folly."

For truly from all sorts of Herbes and Flowers we may draw matter at all times not only to magnifie the Creator that hath given them such diversities of formes, sents and colours, that the most cunning Worke-man cannot imitate, and such vertues and properties, that although wee know many, yet many more lye hidden and unknowne, but many good instructions to our selves.

—John Parkinson, *A Garden of Pleasant Flowers*

Sowing Directly in the Garden

John Parkinson ([1629] 1907) also had it right when he suggested the soil should "neede to bee well cleansed from all annoyances" before planting annual seed directly into the garden soil. Rocks and weeds have no place in a good flower bed and it is only by constant attention to their removal that a good soil will result. My own gardens seem to grow stones over the winter and flowers in the summer; every year I pick the former in the spring and the latter in the fall. Nothing ruins your day like trying to hand-cultivate a bed with a small tool and continually thwacking that tool off rocks. Your wrist and arm soon tire of the sport.

IT IS WELL KNOWN that gardeners, before they either sow a bed in the kitchen-garden, or a patch of flower seeds in the flower-garden, generally "firm the ground," as they call it, by beating it well with the back of the spade, or pressing it with a saucer of a flower-pot; and there can be no doubt that this is done in order that the seeds may be firmly imbedded in the soil.

—JANE LOUDON, *Gardening for Ladies and Companion to the Flower Garden*

Some gardeners sow seeds directly into the soil immediately after cultivating. I have found—and the old-timers back this up—that firming the soil before planting is a far better practice and will result in higher germination rates. Loose soil allows the seed to settle into the cracks and get too deep for easy germination. A firm soil is needed to prevent this. Some Victorian gardeners used a shuffle step across the plot to compress the soil with their boots while others recommended patting the soil with the back of a spade. Mrs. Loudon recommended the spade as well as the back of a flowerpot saucer. If you only have a few seeds to sow, a saucer might be a very useful, although a cumbersome tool. Your hands would serve equally well.

THE PRINCIPLE POINTS to be attended to in sowing seeds are, first, to prepare the ground so that the young and tender roots thrown out by the seeds may easily penetrate into it; secondly, to fix the seeds firmly in the soil; thirdly, to cover them, so as to exclude the light, which impedes vegetation, and to preserve a sufficiency of moisture round them to encourage it; and, fourthly, not to bury them so deeply as either to deprive them of the beneficial influence of the air, or to throw any unnecessary impediments in the way of their ascending shoots.

—JANE LOUDON, *Gardening for Ladies and Companion to the Flower Garden*

More seeds in the garden die from being buried too deeply than from almost any other cause. The rule of thumb used in our own gardens is to only cover the seed to its own depth. If the seed is ¼ inch across, then it gets buried ¼ inch down. If it is ¹/₃₂ inch across, then this is the depth of the covering it receives. Once the seed is sown and covered, it is immediately watered with a very fine mist nozzle or a watering can with a fine rose (a "rose" is the business end of the watering can with all the holes in it; roses come in different grades—from fine to coarse sprays). This watering is essential to ensure the seed is in full contact with the soil and that adequate moisture is present to encourage germination. Seedbeds have to be

WATERING CAN

kept constantly moist until germination occurs and the roots start to penetrate the soil. Once the seedlings have two pairs of true leaves showing (true leaves are the leaves of the mature plant and do not include the initial pair of seed leaves) then discontinue constant watering and start a regular garden-watering regime. The amount recommended for the average garden bed is 1 to 1 ½ inches of water per week. Inches of water are easily measured by placing a large plastic tub (the kind margarine comes in—wider than it is deep—works well) in the garden under the sprinkler pattern and measuring the depth of the water in the tub. Any combination of natural rainfall and sprinkler water should equal 1 to 1 ½ inches of water per week. Again, a common recommendation is to apply this amount of water in two equal amounts of ¾ inch. Tuesday and Friday waterings or other similarly spaced applications are ideal. I prefer sprinkling to hand watering because the sprinkler is much more democratic and ensures all plants get equal amounts of water. It is also much more reliable than I am; it waters the garden thoroughly without taking coffee breaks or going too fast to get on to other tasks. Besides, if the sprinkler is doing the work for me, I feel perfectly justified in taking a short break to supervise its activities, preferably with a good cup of tea in a comfortable chair out of its watering path. The garden and its flowers are for enjoyment—not for compulsion.

DON'T WATER PLANTS during the day because the water droplets will burn the plants.

— OLD WIVES' TALE

Watering in the morning is preferable since it gives the leaves a chance to dry in the heat of the sun. The old wives' tale which warns not to water during the day because the droplets will act as magnifying glasses is exactly that—an old wives' tale. The angles of refraction are all wrong to burn plants. You still shouldn't water at midday because more than 5o percent of the liquid will evaporate before it gets used by the roots; it is a waste of good water, but it won't burn your plants. Regularly watering at night may lead to an increase in fungus diseases, especially in plants that are disease-prone. Powdery mildew will be more of a problem in monarda, phlox and lilac for example if they are regularly watered at night. Damp, dark conditions are the delight of many fungus and bacterial diseases. Invest in drip irrigation lines instead of overhead sprinklers if night watering is to be the rule rather than the exception. Drip irrigation puts the water into the soil without wetting the leaves.

Spring Versus Fall Sowing

There is a wonderful gardening belief that sowing hardy annuals in the fall is as good as sowing them early in the spring. Well, maybe. A recent bit of research showed that mice and ants ate more than 9o percent of the seeds in gardens and fields before these seeds ever had a chance to germinate. Without the mice and ants, every garden and field would be overrun with weeds and plants—a jungle of almost uncontrollable growth. There is a balance to the garden that we sometimes fail to see and appreciate. While gardeners worry about the ants in their garden and on their flowers, these same ants are reducing weed populations. Nature indeed works in mysterious ways if we let it.

EVERYONE KNOWS THAT the seeds of hardy annuals may be sown in the open ground in August and September, and that the resultant plants will be sturdier and will come into flower earlier than those we sow in the spring.

— VITA SACKVILLE-WEST, *More for Your Garden*

There is one thing about handling garden-sown seeds that bothers most gardeners, myself included. When faced with success, we have too many precious seedlings in a confined space and some must be removed. If we have planned ahead, the seed will have been sown thinly enough so that the adult plants will not crowd each other out. I confess that I have never been able to trust to obtaining perfect germination and obtaining plants where I want them. I overseed. I put too many seeds in each spot to ensure I get my hardy annuals where I want them. This means every year I am faced with the necessary task of thinning out excess seedlings. If I fail to do so, I raise thin, weak, straggly specimens that neither do the plant or myself proud. It is only when I screw up my courage to weed out perfectly good plants, leaving only the strongest and most perfectly situated, that I ensure myself of a good flower show and the title of gardener. Do transplant some of the extra seedlings into holes where poor germination occurred (water them in thoroughly after transplanting), but be prepared to ruthlessly discard any surplus.

UNLESS THE FLOWERING SEASON is to be of short duration, I have yet to see a satisfactory plan for a perennial garden without annuals to complete its bloom.

— LOUISE SHELTON, *Continuous Bloom in America*

FALL OR SPRING SOWING?

Do annuals sown in the fall bloom faster than the same annuals sown in the spring, as Vita Sackville-West (1955) suggests? It depends on when you sow your annuals in the spring. Seeds will not germinate until the conditions are right. Soil temperature and moisture have to be at the proper level. If a gardener sows the seeds at the correct time, when soil temperatures are warm enough—our hardy annual

MALMAISON BALSAM

seeds start germinating sporadically around 60° F and truly launch themselves in numbers around 68 to 70° F—then both the overwintered seeds and the newly planted seeds will germinate at the same time. Naturally, if the gardener waits an extra day or three after the soil has warmed appropriately (say, waiting for the weekend to sow the seed), then the overwintered seed will germinate before the spring-sown seed. I reluctantly contradict Vita Sackville-West, a well-respected British garden writer, when I point out that spring-planted seeds are in a much reduced danger of being eaten by mice and ants when compared to fall sown. I also find that garden-sown seeds—either in spring or fall—are indistinguishable from each other in my own gardens. I do find that hardy annuals that are started in the greenhouse are not as sturdy and healthy as garden-sown plants, even though the greenhouse-sown and transplanted ones may bloom a bit earlier than the garden sown. Also, in colder climates, from Zone 6 on down, many of the hardy annual seeds will die or rot when exposed to freezing temperatures. Seed that survives outdoors in California or Sussex, England, may not be up to a New England or prairie winter.

Pruning/Deadheading

Annual flowers and gardeners have had a silent competition for as long as there have been flower gardens. The plants want to set seeds. The gardeners want extra flowers. If the plants succeed in setting seed, they seem perfectly content and often refuse to produce more flowers. Gardeners therefore keep cutting off the spent flowers before they set seed, hoping the plant will produce more blossoms. Salvia is a perfect example. As long as the gardener continues to cut the fading flowers from the plant before they go to seed, the plant will produce more blossoms.

As soon as the plant sets seed, the gardener needs to start dreaming of next year's flowers, because there will be precious few produced by this plant during the remainder of this season. Pruning off the old blossom creates new growth, and it is this new growth that produces the new blooms. Removing the dying or fading flowers before they set seed is called deadheading. I have always admired this simple term for a necessary task; there is no wasted verbiage, no pretension of finer things. It is a strong word for a good garden practice. Deadheading—do it.

Beginners will often ask where to make the deadhead cut. Generally, try to cut back to a growing leaf or another flower-producing stem. Do not leave a stub or stalk

DEADHEADING
ANNUALS

sticking up above the leaf canopy. Besides being ugly, the stalk will die back, leaving an unsightly brown stalk. The stalk may, especially if the plant is under stress, create a dead zone further back into the plant. Cutting at a leaf node and removing the stalk allows the plant to recover and set new growth and new flowers. Some writers will tell you to always make your cuts at an angle across the stem whenever you prune. I have not found an advantage either to the angled or the straight cut. It is more important to get the job done than it is to worry about the angle of the cut.

HALF-HARDY ANNUALS

Annual flower seeds are easily pleased. Give them a damp, warm place and they will inevitably start to grow. With any luck at all for the seed, the gardener will also provide a weed-free soil, light, and food so the young seedling will get a successful start in life. Different writers promote their favorite containers; these range from old egg cartons to the most modern of portable greenhouses. In my experience, flower seeds will grow in almost any container; it is the conditions of growth which gardener provides that spell the difference between success and failure. The number one cause of half-hardy annuals failing to germinate is burying the seed too deeply. Just as with hardy annuals, the seed should be buried no deeper than its width. Half-hardy annual seed tends to be smaller than hardy annual seed. Over the years I produced flowers in the nursery business, I experimented with germinating them in different ways. I generally found that if the soil was kept damp and warm, I did not have to cover smaller half-hardy seeds (pansies being the major exception). The larger seeds would also germinate equally well without covering, but their subsequent growth was faster if they had a slight covering of soil to assist their roots in establishing and orienting themselves. Pansies require a period of dark to help their germination, so cover the seed slightly with soil or cover the seedling tray with a dark covering. Very tiny seeds, such as begonia and petunia, were never covered with soil. Note that if the soil is allowed to dry out at all during the germination process, the seeds will do slightly better when covered. The layer of soil gives an extra bit of protection against drying out. Alternately, keep the soil consistently damp by covering the seed flat with plastic or some other transparent material.

Use sterilized soil as a seed-starting medium. The easiest way to do this is to use an artificial soil mixture, available at your local garden center. Soil mixtures that contain real soil or compost of any kind should be sterilized before use as seed-starting soils, even if fresh out of a bag. You can use the oven — twenty-five minutes at 325° F should bake a good, if odiferous, large cake pan of potting soil. You can use the microwave — fifteen minutes at the high setting should do the job — or you can use a very simple system of boiling water. Fill the pots with the soil mix, leaving ½ inch of rim showing at the top of the pot. Slowly, very slowly, pour boiling water into the pot — as if you were watering the plants — until the hot water is freely running out the bottom of the pot. Allow the pot to cool before sowing and you will not be likely to have any soil-borne problems.

GROUP OF PANSIES

EVERY RIPE SEED in a dry state is a concentration of carbon, which, when dissolved by moisture, and its particles set in motion by heat, is in a fit state to combine with the oxygen in the atmosphere, and thus to form the carbonic acid gas which is the nourishment of the expanding plant.

— JANE LOUDON, *Gardening for Ladies and Companion to the Flower Garden*

Despite Mrs. Loudon's theory that carbonic gas would feed her seedlings, I feed my germinated seedlings with a very dilute plant food. Normally, once the seedlings have two true leaves, they are put on a diet of one-quarter strength starter plant food of a 10-52-10 formula applied once a week. Different companies will slightly alter the formula but anything with a higher second number than the first and third will be fine. This concentration and formula are kept until the seedling is transplanted into a larger pot to continue developing. After transplanting, change the formula to a 20-20-20 (or similar equal number formula) concentration and slowly increase it week by week. The fourth week after transplanting, you should see the thriving plants being fed at the recommended strength on the fertilizer label.

Naturally, when you get to start the majority of your plants in a greenhouse, providing enough light is not one of life's little gardening worries. If your homegrown seedlings start to stretch out, looking long and leggy, the major culprit is a lack of light. Increase the light levels by adding lights, adding even more lights, or lowering the lights closer to the crop. Spindly seedlings never perform as well in the garden as their shorter, stockier cousins. Sometimes if enough light is available a room that is too hot will create a taller, spindly plant. Normally half-hardy annuals prefer a germination *soil* temperature of 72° F but a growing-on *air* temperature of 62° to 64° F. A recipe to ensure spindly plants is to provide too low a light level and too high a room temperature. Do remember that soil temperatures will be approximately 10° F lower than the air temperature around them.

Transplanting

THE FIRST POINT is to avoid injuring the roots, and it is only necessary to consider the construction and uses of these most important organs to perceive how impossible it is for the plant to thrive, unless they are in a perfectly healthy state.

— JANE LOUDON, *Gardening for Ladies and Companion to the Flower Garden*

Mrs. Loudon has it almost exactly right. The roots are very important in transplanting half-hardy annuals from their seedling trays to the growing-on pots. The more root you can take with you, the better the seedling will recover from the transplant shock and the faster it will start to grow again. My experience in the greenhouse does, however, point to another factor that beginning gardeners sometimes miss. The plant stem is particularly vulnerable and fragile while being transplanted. The vast majority of transplant loss or subsequent weakened growth comes from stem damage, not root damage. Bruising the stem results in poor transportation of nutrients back and forth between the leaves and roots; this leads to poor initial growth. Sometimes the plant will grow out of this damage; more often it

will either die or grow poorly. To avoid stem damage, handle the transplants by the topmost
leaves. Even if these leaves are damaged or torn
while transplanting, the plant will quickly produce new ones and will continue growing.

HANDLING TRANSPLANTS

Disease Control in Transplants

The major disease that home gardeners see with their transplants is damping off. This complex of diseases attacks the stem
at the soil line, rotting it and causing the plant to collapse. The
cause of this problem is a soil-borne organism that occurs under
conditions of poorly sterilized soil, overcrowded seedlings, low
temperatures, and overwatering. The last three are the major
culprits, with overcrowding and subsequent lack of air around
the stem being the most important. Either sow the seeds quite
thinly in the pot or thin them out as they germinate to prevent
overcrowding and damping off. If seed leaves overlap one
another as they germinate there are too many seedlings in the
pot and an invitation to damping off has been offered.

Sometimes, despite the best intentions and the best practices, damping off gets established in the pot. Seedlings collapse
and the crop appears to be ruined. To salvage the crop, first
remove all dead and dying seedlings. Then crush a clove or two
of garlic, put the mush into a saucepan with several cups of
water, and slowly simmer for a few minutes to draw the oils out
of the garlic. Allow the water to cool, then pour it over the pot to

thoroughly soak all seedlings and the soil. I have heard some authors recommend straining the garlic chunks out and using the water in a mister to spray the seedlings. I've tried this method but I can never seem to remove all the tiny bits of garlic. My sprayers constantly clog up. I can say that the lukewarm garlic water, chunks and all, does a good job of fighting damping off.

Sanitation is the key to avoiding seedling problems. Keep pots clean, soils sterilized, and seedlings well spaced out and warm. These rules for commercial growers should be adopted by amateurs as well.

Growing On

"Growing on" is one of the great gardening terms we all love to throw around. It rolls off the tongue and instantly enhances the status of the speaker. If you are "growing on" a plant, you are an established seed master, a confirmed successful transplanter, a person with a small nursery of plants; indeed, you become an instant expert just by using the term. "Growing on" just means to grow the plant to a larger size, but once you use the term and perform the task, you join the ranks of the established gardener and forever leave the beginners behind.

Getting the seedling to grow on into a large plant is a simple process but one that sometimes confuses beginning gardeners. To begin with, seeds of the half-hardy annuals will need to be transplanted from their seedling pots into their own containers if they are to achieve enough growth for spring transplanting. It

is this extra growth that enables us to ensure that fibrous bego-
nias, seed-started geraniums, or the other half-hardy plants grow
large enough to go out into the garden and flower during the
frost-free garden months. The smaller the container being used
to grow the plant to garden size, the more work and attention the
plant will demand. A plant put in one of the small cell packs
commonly found in garden centers will demand much more frequent and regular watering than will its cousin transplanted into
its own four-inch pot. Plants crowded into cell packs will require
much more ventilation as they grow larger or damping off will
rear its ugly head again. In my own garden, I use three-and-a-
half-inch or four-inch pots to grow on my seedlings for garden
transplanting. This size pot gives the plant adequate soil for root
growth. The pots are large enough to support the weight and
top growth of most half-hardy annuals, so by the time the last
frost has left, my annuals are large enough to plant and, usually blooming, ready to give instant color to the garden. I also
encourage my half-hardy annuals by spacing them on the growing bench so that the edges of their leaves are just touching. I
used to start them tightly together and move them farther and
farther apart as they grew, but, being a lazy gardener, I figured
out how far they would grow and I now space them at their
mature distance apart when I transplant them. As a very rough
rule of thumb, find a quarter of the mature size of the plant and
separate half-hardy plants by this distance. Your own gardening
practices may increase or decrease this space, but this is a good
starting distance and one you can modify with experience.

Adequate light, temperature, and fertility are critical for the proper development of the half-hardy annual. Sometimes, though, a mistake is made and the plant gets too long and leggy. There are two steps to remedy this situation. The first is to figure out why it happened so that you can avoid the mistake in the future. Not enough light, not enough or too much feeding, too hot a growing temperature, too much crowding, too early sowing – all these things will create a tall, overgrown seedling. The second step is to solve the problem, and the remedy is as close as the nearest pair of kitchen scissors. Cut anywhere from one-third to one-half of the top of the plant right off. Normally, a too-tall plant also comes with dying bottom leaves, particularly if crowding has caused the stretching. Clean off any dead or dying leaves. The pruned-off tops can be treated as cuttings; follow the directions given in Chapter 2 for rooting success. New growth on the potted annuals will come from the leaf axils, the place where the leaf attaches to the stem. The annual, newly reduced to its proper height, will sprout new leaves and shoots, thicken up, and become more like the plant you see in your mind's eye. If your seedlings were crowded, increase the spacing so the new bushy growth will have room to grow without touching its bench neighbor. It will take approximately four weeks from this drastic pruning until the plant has fully recovered and filled out. This trick of top pruning is a common one, used by many gardeners to thicken up their plants. As most annuals bloom

GERANIUM
CUTTING

on new growth, the more new growth created by the heavy pruning, the more blossoms the plant will produce. Gardeners routinely top cut their annuals to thicken them up, not just to
rejuvenate them after a growing on misadventure.

One of the first plants to be bedded-out extensively was the 'Tom Thumb'
pelargonium or geranium as it was then more commonly called; it was a dwarf
scarlet, and was considered to be of great beauty till the better varieties were
introduced. Then followed verbeneas, calceolarias, and other flowers, which
could be kept as cuttings through the winter, and then be planted out when
summer weather made it safe to do so.

— Henry A. Bright, *The English Flower Garden*

Vita Sackville-West (1955) put it so well: "The brief and
gaudy blaze produced by the half-hardies enlivens the summer garden." A gaudy blaze of color is to be recommended
in many gardens.

Designing for Annual Gardens

Garden writers who love plants generally get themselves into
trouble when recommending designs and design tips to their
readers. The trouble starts with the question of how to fit all the
plants we love to grow into the small space of our own gardens.
Some gardeners resort to an ever-increasing construction project—the new-bed-a-year syndrome. Others try to discipline
themselves to only certain plants or special colors. As a friend
said, "Too many plants, too little time."

RATIONAL PLANTING, ALLOWING
SPACE FOR NATURAL DISTRIBU-
TION OF ROOTS, THE CROWN
OF THE PLANT LEVEL WITH
SURFACE OF SOIL

AN EXAMPLE OF BAD PLANTING,
WITH ROOTS CRAMPED IN TOO
SMALL A HOLE

Luckily there are some guidelines that assist us in creating those wonderful garden pictures we all love to dream on. The following suggestions will give you something to think about when you plant your annuals next spring.

Formal Planting

Planting annuals in straight rows is formal planting. Seeing the line of soldier-straight yellow marigolds or red and white petunias marching up a driveway has become a bit of a cliché in many urban communities. Taking this single line one step further and adding several different kinds of annuals to create colored patterns is called "carpet bedding." Carpet bedding was taken to extremes by the Victorian gardeners of England. When the inevitable backlash arrived, it did so with an effect that we

still feel today. Today, carpet bedding is normally only seen
in parks or formal gardens that are large enough — and brave
enough — to tackle the huge maintenance bills and plant cost of
such a display.

THIS MAY BE well enough; but who wants flower-beds to look like carpets? They
may strike you at first as being ingenious, and even pretty, but the feeling is at
once followed by a sense of their essential debasement as regards gardening.

HENRY A. BRIGHT, *The English Flower Garden*

Does carpet bedding have a place in the home garden? It
surely does if it is the desire of the resident gardener. There are
several guidelines for success with carpet bedding that need be
taken to heart by gardeners determined to use half-hardy annuals in massed plantings.

Plant the annuals at the recommended spacing. Too far
apart creates huge holes and invitations for weeds to germinate and grow. Too close together creates a mass of leaves and
poor air circulation, resulting in disease and the need for
increased pruning.

Maintain the planting. Nothing looks so grubby as a poorly
maintained mass planting of half-hardy annuals. Deadhead
regularly and rigorously. Otherwise, the eye will find the fading
and rotting blooms almost before anything else — to the detri-
ment of the garden show. Prune rank growth. Any annual that
begins to grow too large or too quickly needs to be pruned back.
This pruning back will also thicken up the growth. Feed and

CARPET BEDDING—CREATING A PATTERN WITH PLANT
LEAVES AND FLOWERS—IS A LABOR-INTENSIVE FLORAL
DISPLAY. INSTALL THE SAME PLANT IN SIMILARLY
SHAPED SPACES TO CREATE A PATTERN.

water regularly to assist the plant's restoration and continued production of blooms.

Color and beauty are in the eye of the beholder. Enjoy your garden, even if other gardeners do not appreciate your color sense. Choosing flower colors and designing the garden are far beyond the scope of this book. Even our gardening predecessors could not agree on what made a pleasing combination. If you are like the gardeners who have gone before you, your tastes will change from year to year and your gardens will reflect this change. Enjoy your current garden for the joy it brings you, and ignore the advice of gardeners such as Bright (1881), who, not mincing words, accused half of all English gardeners of being "colour-blind." This kind of rhetoric makes great garden writing but not great gardening advice.

It really would sometimes appear that half our English gardeners must be colour-blind. The gaudiest and most glaring contrasts pain instead of gratifying the eye, with their crude patches of pink and red and blue and yellow.

— Henry A. Bright, *The English Flower Garden*

Planting in Drifts

One technique that can be copied from the perennial border is to plant our annual flowers in "drifts." Both hardy and half-hardy annuals can be treated this way to great effect. In essence, the gardener picks the point of view that the garden will be seen from. The flowers are then planted in swaths at roughly a forty-five-degree angle to this point of view. Each drift looks better if

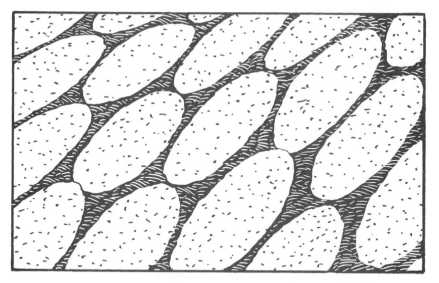

PLANTING IN DRIFTS—SEEDS SOWN IN LONG OVALS,
ONE VARIETY TO EACH OVAL

it is at least three times longer than its width. Avoid squares or blocks of color in this kind of design. There will be more impact if the patches of color are longer. Planting in this way creates wide bands of color that interact across the entire point of view of the garden. If the plants are arranged from short in front to taller in the rear, the flowers and foliage of the shorter forms in the front will block out any unsightly stems of those plants toward the rear. Using annuals allows the garden to be in full bloom for almost the entire summer, giving a marvelous show for little investment. All suggestions for maintenance of formal carpet bedding apply to these informal annual gardens as well.

Mixed Assortments

Some gardeners prefer not to do the work of garden design, of planning the colors and plant varieties that will occupy the garden. An easy method is to mix several packets of seed into one bunch and sow the seed as if it were one kind. The resulting mix will be serendipitous. If seeds of similar heights are mixed together, plant the short mix at the front and the taller mixes toward the rear of the garden for an easy garden design. You can custom design your own mix from your favorite flowers. Alternatively, some seed houses sell these mixes already packaged.

One border may be given up to annuals, and it is no bad plan to mix the seeds of some twenty varieties, and let them grow together as they will.

— Henry A. Bright, *The English Flower Garden*

Saving Seed

There are many reasons why the average gardener should save his or her own flower seeds and only one reason why not to. Let us get the single negative reason out of the way first. Hybrid seeds are the result of complex breeding programs, and the inescapable fact is that the offspring of these hybrids seldom totally resemble their parents. Oh, to be sure, the seeds can be saved and they will grow, but they will seldom produce exactly the color or number of blooms as were in the parent plant. If you are a seed saver, do not grow hybrid plants. There are enough hardy annuals that are open-pollinated (non-hybrid) to stock bigger gardens than yours or mine in our lifetimes. Collect and save these instead of the hybrids.

There are almost too many reasons why a gardener should save their own seeds to mention in a single book. I save my own for the satisfaction it gives me and to ensure I can obtain the plants I want to grow for my own garden. Many of the plants I want to grow are not available at local garden centers or hardware store seed-racks. To obtain the particular form of annual Japanese aster I like, I now save my own garden seed. I can also control the color of the garden. If I only save and replant the seed from the red aster flowers, sooner or later every aster in the garden will be red.

The greatest defect with our flower-growing is the stinginess of it.
—Liberty Hyde Bailey, *Manual of Gardening*

Saving seed is quite easy. Don't deadhead a few blossoms of the best-looking plant in the garden. Allow those blossoms to set seed instead. When these seedheads are dry, the seed can be easily harvested by hand and put into an envelope. I make an effort to totally seal the envelope as I have discovered the little unglued edges allow the smaller seeds to escape and leak out. The tape dispenser is a regular visitor to the garden on my seed collecting forays. I use regular business size envelopes and write the name of the plant and the year I collected the seed on the outside of the envelope. While I have a good memory, it is too short to recall the contents of each envelope without the prompting of my penciled notes. I store the seed in the crisper of the refrigerator until the following spring when I sow it again outside. The seed could be stored with equal success in any other location as long as it is kept cool and dry.

I do try to clean the seed before I store it. There will always be chaff, dirt, and often insects or their victims inside the drying seedheads. Remove all extraneous material, leaving only the seed for next year's garden. There is a good chance this extra material will rot over the winter, ruining the seeds and spoiling your dreams. The cleaner the seed, the better it will store.

Hardy annuals are wonderful plants in the garden. Grow them, collect them, and enjoy them. If you read the names of the authors who have supported their use, you will realize you are in good company.

DEAR READER: IN closing my descriptive and priced list of seeds I wish but to say that I have endeavored to give only truthful descriptions and honest illustrations. I have not attempted to induce sales by over praise. I would rather not have your orders than to get them by deception. As to prices, you will agree with me that they are low; while I assure you that the quality of the seeds is high. I do not handle cheap seeds. My seeds speak their own praise. All I ask is a fair trial. . . . Let me hear from you soon.

— GEO W. PARK, *Park's Floral Guide 1900*

CHAPTER FOUR

BULB CULTURE

HORA FUGIT RAPIDE LETHUMQ;
INVADIT INERMES

*The hours glide swiftly and the unguarded are
easily surprised.*

—A BOOK OF SUNDIAL MOTTOES

Bulbs are the signal of spring in my garden; the species bulbs burst out of their winter rest in the alpine beds and cheerfully announce that spring has arrived. No matter that in the odd spring they are covered with snow again in a last winter's gasp; they have done their duty and broken winter's grip on the land. I confess I look forward more to the cheerful yellow *Crocus chrysanthus*—normally the first bulb to bloom in my garden—than any other plant for the rest of the summer. That little charmer has won a prominent place in the garden merely by being the first to bloom. As soon as the snow leaves the ground I start looking for its short spears and yellow blooms. In many years, there is still snow on other parts of the garden when its yellow blossoms brighten my day. There is no question that other garden authors have felt the same way over the years. The old books are full of praise for bulbs. From the seventeenth century and John Parkinson to Mrs. Loudon's nineteenth-century treatise, we all have waxed poetic about bulbs and their place in the garden.

In this solitary coming forth, which is far more beautiful when we chance to see it thus amidst the melting snow rather than on the dark bare earth, the kind little flower, however it may gladden us, seems itself to wear an aspect almost of sorrow. Yet wait another day or two till the clouds have broken and its brave hope is accomplished, and the solitary one has become a troop, and all down the garden amongst the shrubs the little white bunches are dancing gaily in the breeze.

—John Ruskin, as quoted in *The English Flower Garden*

Grow bulbs for their spring charm, their summer fragrance, and their versatility in the cutting garden. Indeed, grow bulbs and you will be in fine gardening company: from Parkinson to Sackville-West, bulb growing is a fine gardening tradition.

Rules for Growing Bulbs

There are three rules for growing a good bulb. The first is to make sure there is excellent drainage so the bulb does not suffer from excess water. Overwatering bulbs or growing them in heavy—or clay—soils causes bulbs to fade away. First they come up without their bloom and then they simply disappear from the garden. Often rodents are blamed for this disappearance rather than the true culprits, garden soil or overwatering.

A good compost for the growth of common bulbs is one part clean sand, one part leaf-mould or rich garden-loam, and one part well-rotted cow-dung.

—Edward Sprague Rand, Jr., *Bulbs: A Treatise on Hardy and Tender Bulbs and Tubers*

The recipe given by Mr. Rand for good bulb-growing soil—the British call any improved garden soil compost—is a perfect example of a soil that has good drainage, with one-third of the soil being sand and one-third being good loam or leaf mold. Remember, though, that if you have to replace soil in heavy clay in order to grow bulbs, it is important to not create a "bathtub effect" in the garden by ensuring that the area being modified is well drained. See Chapter 1 for drainage discussion.

Rand also speaks to the very important second rule for growing good bulbs. In his recipe, the third component is "well-rotted cow-dung." Because bulbs are underground and out of sight for the bulk of the year, gardeners forget that they have specific needs for food. Every summer the bulbs have to replace the energy spent producing leaves and flowers, and it is our job as gardeners to give them the necessary nutrients. A generous composting of the garden each spring will allow enough nutrients to reach bulb depth to keep them happy. Another option is to give bulbs a liquid feed immediately after the plants flower to ensure they receive adequate nutrition for their growing phase.

THE STRONGER AND MORE VIGOROUS the leaves are, the stronger will be the bulb, and, consequently, the larger and finer the bloom. Neglect of this first rule is the cause of most failures. To bloom the bulb the first year is easy: you only have to develop what another has prepared: the success can hardly be called your own. But if, the second year, you can produce as fine, or even finer flowers, you may well claim to possess skill in bulb-culture.

—EDWARD SPRAGUE RAND, JR., *Bulbs: A Treatise on Hardy and Tender Bulbs and Tubers*

The last and probably most important rule is to grow the foliage, not the flower. Too many gardeners want to hurry the bulb along, to cut off the foliage so as to plant annuals in that space or tidy up the mass of flopping leaves left after the blooms have finished. In this it is good to remember a poster my wife has above the door in her painting studio: NEATNESS IS FOR LESSER MORTALS. Neatness in bulbs does not count; an untidy garden is a productive garden because the bulb leaves are storing energy for next year's bloom. For this is what they are doing, and if the leaves are cut off too early, before they have yellowed and started to fade, then the bulb has not yet finished its regrowth and next year's bloom will suffer. Grow the foliage well and the flower will take care of itself. Growing the leaves is a fine point to remember because it applies to all bulbs, whether spring or summer blooming. Small tips such as cutting the leaves off rather than pulling them off when they are yellowed and faded are also important to remember. Pulling, always so tempting, tends to dislodge shallow or smaller bulbs, and the gardener may wind up with a handful of bulbs on the end of the old leaves.

THE PRIMARY RULE in bulb-culture is, *grow the foliage well*.

—EDWARD SPRAGUE RAND, JR., *Bulbs: A Treatise on Hardy and Tender Bulbs and Tubers*

Deadheading the spent flowers is another way of ensuring the leaves do their job. If the spent flower stalks are not cut off, the bulb will try to set seed. While setting seed is good for the bulb and the gardener wishing to experiment, it does take more

growing energy and time to do this. A bulb that is not dead-
headed in our garden will stay green and growing for an extra
week or two when compared to its shorn neighbors. Another
method of speeding up the garden availability and making sure
the bulbs have finished their growth period before the annuals
or perennials take their turn is to plant only the early-flowering
bulb varieties. Too many gardeners plant late-flowering tulips,
for example, and then get frustrated because they occupy garden
space when it is time to plant the annuals. Switch from late- to
early-flowering varieties and this problem largely disappears.

Another design option to be considered is to use an entire
class of plants, such as iris or anemone, in the same garden spot
to provide a very long season of bloom. For example, if, the gardener plants perennial as well as the annual forms of anemone,
using Parkinson's suggestions, a very long season of bloom can
be achieved. Of anemone he wrote,

The ordinary time to plant Anemones is
most commonly in August, which will beare
flower some peradventure before Winter,
but most usually in February, March and
Aprill, few or none of them abiding untill
May; but if you will keepe some rootes out
of the ground unplanted, untill February,
March and Aprill, and plant some at one
time, and some at another, you shall have
them beare flower according to their planting, those that shall be planted in February,

SIBERIAN IRIS

will flower about the middle or end of May, and so the rest accordingly after that manner: And thus you may have the pleasure of these plants out of their natural seasons, which is not permitted to be enjoyed in any other that I know, Nature being not so prone to bee furthered by art in other things as in this (Parkinson [1629] 1907).

In short, stagger your plantings of annual bulbs to encourage a longer season of bloom.

Planting Bulbs

Planting bulbs is pretty simple stuff. Dig a hole, place the bulb in the hole, cover it up (Loudon [1843] 1851). Gardening rarely gets simpler than that. Simple yet enjoyable. Summer bulbs spring immediately to life, providing us with an abundance of blooms and fragrances, while the fall-planted perennial bulbs teach us about patience before easing our way into spring. There are only a few questions to be answered about growing a good bulb display. Luckily our gardening predecessors have answered them for us.

Depth of Planting

The major question is how deep should the hole be dug. The first rule of thumb is that the crown of the bulb goes down 1 inch for every inch of length of the bulb. So if a bulb such as a large daffodil is 3 inches long, then I would plant this bulb 3 inches deep. Since planting bulbs is not rocket science, I do not question if the hole is only 2 inches deep or actually 4 inches deep. The bulbs have never complained. I plant small bulbs according to this direction and they usually wind up 1 inch deep. Bulb seedlings that I start myself get put into the ground at the same depth they were found in the seedling pot.

IN PLANTING IN THE OPEN GROUND, the general rule is that the crown of the bulb should be placed an inch below the surface: if in a situation, however, where the bulbs would be liable to be thrown out by the frost, an inch and a half will not be too deep. The larger the bulb, the deeper it should be planted.

—EDWARD SPRAGUE RAND, JR., *Bulbs: A Treatise on Hardy and Tender Bulbs and Perennials*

When bulbs are seedlings, they have an interesting ability to pull themselves deeper into the ground until they arrive at their genetically determined flowering depth. The young seedling produces a fleshy root that anchors itself well and then shrivels up in the fall; this shriveling pulls the small bulblet deeper into the soil. A new fleshy root is produced every spring. The bulb does not start to bulk up to flowering size and stop producing these specialized fleshy roots until it reaches the proper depth.

The last comment about planting bulbs has to do with tulips. These bulbs are so often eaten by predators that I have started planting them at least 8 to 12 inches deep in my garden. This deep planting has not affected their flowering or flowering time. As long as the ground is fertile and I allow the leaves to finish their growth cycle, the bulbs stay healthy and happy at that depth.

PARROT TULIP

Methods of Planting

Friends of mine plant their bulbs the old-fashioned way. They excavate large bushel-basket-sized holes, lay the bulbs in neat rows on the bottom of each hole, and then backfill with the garden soil and generous amounts of bonemeal and compost. I think this is truly admirable of them but, being a lazy gardener, I much prefer the bulb auger. This electric drill attachment resembles a large wood drill and quite easily excavates a three-inch-wide hole—exactly sized for any bulb—in the ground . It will dig up to 12 inches deep and the only requirement is a long extension cord to keep the drill turning. Available at many garden centers or mail-order gardening stores, this auger saves a great deal of labor and trouble. Simply drill the hole, drop in the bulb, scuff the dirt back down the hole with your foot and the job is done. No bending or stooping and no sore back. It does lack the elegance of the bushel-basket-sized hole, but no gardening practice is perfect.

THESE DOE FLOWER some earlier, some later, for three whole moneths together at the least, therein adorning out a garden most gloriously, in that being but one kinde of flower, it is so full of variety, as no other (except the Daffodils, which yet are not comparable, in that they yeeld not that alluring pleasant variety) doe the like besides.

—JOHN PARKINSON, *A Garden of Pleasant Flowers*

Many gardeners prefer bulb dibbles to the shovel or auger. These gardeners, planting on bended knee, are to be congratulated for maintaining the use of this excellent, if antique, tool.

DIBBLE

For the uninitiated, a dibble is a short, pointed stick that you poke into the ground to make a hole. You then drop the bulb into the hole. As one whose knees have started complaining about the cold ground under them, I very much prefer the standing system of the auger. Other gardeners use bulb planters, which consists of a metal circle that is plunged into the ground, twisted, and pulled back out to remove a plug of soil. The mechanics of this tool have always defied me, but I am sure that it makes perfect sense to those who use it.

Planting spring-flowering bulbs takes place in the fall and there are always several problems associated with this. The first is that the bulbs either arrive too late or are put on a shelf and then discovered after frost has hardened the soil. If the frost is not too deep, the bulbs can be planted anyway. Give them a thorough soaking afterward with a garden hose to set them in. The watering is necessary; it definitely increases the survival rate of late-planted bulbs.

In one instance, a lot of hyacinths and crocus, received very late, were planted in the frozen ground (the holes being made with a crowbar), and the next spring showed a fine lot of flowers, but little later than or inferior to, those planted earlier.

— Edward Sprague Rand, Jr., *Bulbs: A Treatise on Hardy and Tender Bulbs and Perennials*

The second situation is that you forget the bulbs until the ground is thoroughly frozen. I have had this happen once or twice myself. I merely potted up the bulbs and put them in a spare refrigerator in the basement. If you maintain the basement, crawl space, or garage above freezing but not above 40° F, then no refrigerator is necessary. Allow the bulbs at least a twelve-week dormancy and then bring them into the warmth of the kitchen for forcing and enjoy the blooms. Plant the bulbs in the garden after all danger of frost has disappeared in the spring. If no space is available for potting the bulbs, they can be left in the crisper of the refrigerator until spring, then planted out as soon as the frost has left the ground. They may or may not flower the first year.

The last situation is when the forgotten bulbs are discovered in the spring, having remained on the shelf for the entire winter. If the bulb is still hard, there is no harm in planting it. If soft, it is rotting and should be discarded. If you're in doubt, plant the bulb. After all, if the bulb is not planted, it will never bloom. If planted, it might bloom.

As we have seen that each bulb has its season of rest, it would follow that all bulbs should, during that season, have nothing to excite their dormant powers and to urge them to growth. With most bulbs, this is afforded by taking them out of the earth, and preserving them in a perfectly dry place, or with many bulbs grown in pots by withholding water and "drying them off."

—Edward Sprague Rand, Jr., *Bulbs: A Treatise on Hardy and Tender Bulbs and Tubers*

Control of Pests and Diseases

In all the years I have been growing bulbs in my garden, the plants have not been overly bothered by pests or diseases. These are almost perfect plants in that regard. I confess that as an author it is very difficult to write polished prose on insect and disease control when you have never had to control these same insects and diseases in your own garden. What other recommendation does a beginning gardener need to start growing bulbs? Rand has put his finger on the most important aspect of bulb culture when it comes to disease control. He writes, "if proper attention is paid to the preparation of soil, and the application of water" then "diseases are not of frequent occurrence in bulb culture" (Rand 1866). This is the way of things for our old authors: get the soil structure right, get the watering and fertility right, and most problems never visit the home garden.

DISEASES ARE NOT OF FREQUENT occurrence in bulb culture, if proper attention is paid to the preparation of soil, and the application of water; and bulbs are subject to the attacks of few insects, if reasonable care is taken. The principal are red spider, green-fly, mealy bug, black, brown, and white scale, mildew and rot.

—EDWARD SPRAGUE RAND, JR., *Bulbs: A Treatise on Hardy and Tender Bulbs and Tubers*

All that said, of course the first time you try to grow a bulb, it will be viciously attacked by all manner of pests and my reputation as an honest gardener and broker of plant information will be in jeopardy. To forestall any discussions along these lines, let me pass along some simple remedies for bulb problems. I hasten to add that these garden pests crop up in other spots in the garden, and you can apply these controls just as easily to other plants as to bulbs.

COPIOUS SYRINGING OF FLOWERING BULBS TO REMOVE PESTS

Insect Pests

Spider mites are sneaky pests whose presence is not normally noted until the damage is extensive and difficult to control. Being the size of a head of a pin and normally resident on the underside of leaves, they are not very visible. Mottling of leaves from their grazing is normally the first sign of their existence. If you turn the leaf over, a sure signal of the existing colony is a faint and delicate webbing. One remedy is insecticidal soap sprayed regularly every few days for a two-week period. Rand (1866) suggests either constant syringing of water or a dusting of sulfur. The syringing of water is particularly effective on indoor forced bulbs, but I cannot speak for the sulfur. I do note that horticultural oils are also currently recommended for spider mites. These light oils suffocate the colony when sprayed from below.

THE REMEDY IS copious syringing, whenever the plants are not in full sunshine. If the foliage can be kept moist for a while, it is certain death to the spider.

—EDWARD SPRAGUE RAND, JR., *Bulbs: A Treatise on Hardy and Tender Bulbs and Tubers*

WHERE THE SPIDER is very plenty, a little flower of sulphur may be dusted over the foliage to advantage.

—EDWARD SPRAGUE RAND, JR., *Bulbs: A Treatise on Hardy and Tender Bulbs and Tubers*

We have talked about aphids in other chapters as being a major garden pest (see page 144 for details of control) so it is not useful to repeat that information here.

Some gardeners tell me that mealy bugs sometimes get established in the leaf axils of their bulb plants. See page 145 for control of mealy bugs. Rand suggests using kerosene oil, a recommendation I have yet to try, but one which might mimic the use of the light horticultural oils. I suspect the horticultural oils would be more effective and easier to apply as a spray rather than kerosene with a "camel's-hair pencil."

THE REMEDY IS to pick or wash off the insects by a careful sponging of the foliage. A touch of kerosene oil, applied to the bug with a very fine camel's-hair pencil, is instant death, and not injurious to the plant.

—EDWARD SPRAGUE RAND, JR., *Bulbs: A Treatise on Hardy and Tender Bulbs and Tubers*

Insecticidal soaps are always a safe and usually effective control for a variety of soft-bodied pests in the home garden.

The key with the soaps is repetition. Spraying every few days
for two weeks is usually much more effective than a single spray.
Soap starts working as soon as it touches the insect. If the soap
does not directly hit the pest, it will not kill it. Once the soap
dries, it is no longer effective. Rand likes soap for a variety of
pests, but he particularly recommends it for brown and white
scale on bulb plants.

THE SIMPLE TREATMENT OF WASHING the foliage and leaf-stalks of the
infested plants with a sponge dipped in weak, warm soapsuds will be found
effectual in all cases.

    —EDWARD SPRAGUE RAND, JR., *Bulbs: A Treatise on Hardy and*
    Tender Bulbs and Tubers

Four-Legged Pests

When it comes to four-legged pests, few gardeners escape the
predation of squirrels and chipmunks. There are several levels
of control for these pests; let me break them down into planting
techniques and flower techniques.

    Deep planting, as has been noted above, deters rodents
from digging up or attacking the fall-planted bulb. The rodents
know it is down there; they just cannot seem to muster the effort
to dig that deep when other food is more plentiful. Disturbed
ground in the fall is a visual clue to squirrels and chipmunks that
a competitor has been digging and burying food. The secret then
is to leave the garden soil looking undisturbed after planting.
Luckily, that is as easy as thoroughly soaking the area with a garden hose. I refer to this as muddifying the ground. All this mud

does several things: It helps settle the newly planted bulbs, it disguises the digging area, and the pests tend to avoid muddy areas if given a choice. If, on the other hand, your planting method is a bushel-basket-sized hole (see above), then it is quite easy to lay a hardware-cloth (wire mesh) screen over the bulbs before backfilling. If a half-inch mesh is used, the squirrels will not be able to dig through to the bulbs, but next spring the shoots will have no difficulty finding their way to the surface. Using my auger to deeply plant my tulips, watering the bulbs in thoroughly, and tugging the mulch back over the planting holes has prevented for many years any fall or winter damage by squirrels and chipmunks in my garden.

BULBS IN THE OPEN AIR are subject to few enemies. Crocus are sometimes eaten by field mice, and mice are also very fond of tiger-flowers; but the depredations thus committed are few.

—EDWARD SPRAGUE RAND, JR., *Bulbs: A Treatise on Hardy and Tender Bulbs and Tubers*

I wish I could say the same thing about spring damage to the flowers themselves. The chipmunks learned to love *Lilium regale* blooms a few years ago and it is a constant battle now to prevent them from stripping the plant right down. We have also had rabbits wander through the garden—our Old English sheepdogs are not great hunters—to strip the leaves off the lily stalks. Chipmunks up top and rabbits along the bottom, and myself as an anguished gardener looking somewhere—anywhere—for a bloom! A gardener has several choices when the bulbs are in

LILIES

The queen of all bulbs has to be the lily. Poets have immortalized this plant and gardeners have succumbed to its charms for ages. As gardeners, we all have our favorite plants, yet I know few gardeners who do not instantly fall in love with a bed of fragrant lilies in full summer splendor. Lilies are visitor magnets in our garden when they come into bloom, and while the gentle whites of the madonna lily and regal lily soothe gardening souls, the shrieking yellow-and-orange oriental and trumpet flowers advertise the garden's excesses. There is no reason why lilies cannot fit into the regular garden scheme of things, taking their place in the herbaceous flower border. In fact, their moment of splendor is best appreciated in the early summer garden when they are supported by the nearby foliage of taller perennial plants. Massing the lilies and surrounding them with strong-stemmed perennials, or even shrubs as E. H. Wilson (1931) recommends, eliminates any staking that more traditional gardeners believe to be necessary with lilies.

AND NOW, INSTEAD OF ORDINARY BEDDING-OUT, let me suggest some garden beds which are far more effective. One is a bed of *Lilum auratum*, with heliotrope to fill up the spaces.

— HENRY A. BRIGHT, *The English Flower Garden*

MOST OF US WHO GARDEN love the Lily overmuch and do it harm unwittingly. Some sorts love woodland soils and the shelter of trees, others love the sun, but all need good drainage and none a rich soil. They are best massed in beds by themselves in association with low-growing shrubs. Keep them away from the heavily manured rose-bed and herbaceous border if you would keep Lilies in health and vigor.

  —E. H. WILSON, *If I Were to Make a Garden*

It is not often I pluck up the courage to disagree with an established expert such as E. H. Wilson but I have been growing my lilies in my herbaceous border for many years and they seem to be doing just fine. Perhaps I do not manure or compost my garden enough to ruin the bulbs but so far, so good. My own lilies seem to agree more with Rand when he suggests that lilies are "rather gross feeders." In any case, the compost and the lilies are both doing fine in our perennial gardens.

MANY LILIES ARE RATHER GROSS FEEDERS, and will bear any manure which is not heating.

  —EDWARD SPRAGUE RAND, JR.,
   Bulbs: A Treatise on Hardy and
   Tender Bulbs and Tubers

The lilies commonly found in garden centers will benefit from a fairly well-defined set of growing conditions. Full sun is an almost universal requirement for success with lilies, although they will toler-

LILIES

continues on next page

ate a bit of late afternoon shade. The more shade they are given, the taller and lankier the plants will grow, increasing their tendency to flop over at the slightest provocation. Lilies also benefit from regular watering, although damp soils or clay soils that hold moisture will quickly lead to rot and the disappearance of the bulb. Therefore, the soil should be well-drained with no standing water during the summer months.

Subject to these warnings the condition of an ideal lily soil are (1) porosity, or free and open drainage, (2) moisture for the root-run, (3) humus, in the form either of leaf-mould, peat, spent hops, or worn-out stable or farmyard manure.

—H. Drysdale Woodcock, K.C.; and J. Coutts, V.M.H.,
Lilies: Their Culture and Management

Lilies do seem to respond to organic matter in the soil. Applying large amounts of organic matter, particularly in new gardens or those with poor soils, is the first step in establishing a successful lily patch. Compost is king here (see chapter 1 for suggestions on soil improvement). I have always mulched my perennial and lily gardens; this not only provides organic matter but it provides a steady soil temperature and even moisture supply that the lily bulb thrives on. In my own garden, the mulch is topped up in the fall after the perennial and lily leaves have been cut back to the ground for winter. Beginners can hardly go wrong if they pay attention to the advice given by Woodcock and Coutts to provide free and open drainage, moisture, and humus for all their lily-growing projects.

bloom. The first is the favorite of animal lovers: to establish a feeding station in the garden designed for squirrels and chipmunks. Heavily feed them the specialized foods they love (sunflower seeds!) and they will not bother your bulb blooms – or at least they will not bother them too much. The second is to purchase one of the foul-tasting spray products from your garden center and regularly apply it to the plant from the time it emerges as a bud until the last petal is falling off. A single spray application will not work. While these pests are persistent, their tastebuds are not all that well developed. If they get a taste of a bud and they like the taste, they will continue to sample all the other buds (even the foul-tasting sprayed buds, which they will leave on the ground uneaten) looking for another good-tasting treat. So early sprays to deter that first taste, as well as consistent and thorough coverage, are necessary to preserve flower buds.

Some garden commentators recommend eliminating the pests using traps and poisons, but while this may fit in with some rural gardening practices, it is surprisingly ineffective in the urban garden. These rodent pests are territorial and if the gardener eliminates one, a newcomer will only be a day or two away from invading the territory and beginning where its dead competitor left off.

Disease Control

If bulbs are left in the ground over the winter, disease ceases to be a problem for gardeners. It is normally only when the bulbs are dug up and stored in the old-fashioned way that disease rears its head. The other conditions that lead to disease are either too much shade or too much water. Both of these garden environments will lead to bulb rot or a slow degradation of flowering, eventually followed by disease and bulb death. It seems that we have to return to the old gardening practices—ensuring good soil, adequate drainage, and sunshine—to maintain the health of our bulbous friends.

I have not been bothered by disease in my bulb gardens, and some of my plantings are more than twenty years old. Friends who have had problems universally agree with Rand when he says that rotting in bulbs is rarely cured and the best remedy is to eliminate the bulbs. It is very likely that the only time home gardeners will see rot on bulbs is when they are being purchased. Do not purchase a bulb with a soft spot on it. This is rot. Avoid bulbs that are damaged or molding in the sales bin. Ripped tunics (the papery covering of the bulb) are not a problem, but other signs of damage are signals to avoid the bulb in question.

If you have a prized annual bulb that develops a bit of rot, sometimes a sharp knife can cut it out. If dusted with sulfur the bulb will survive and regrow into a healthy specimen. While I would never bet the farm on this miraculous recovery, I have brought a few prized bulbs back to the garden after damage and rot had set in. Normally I just throw diseased bulbs away because I do not want to infect other parts of my garden.

CHAPTER FIVE

ROSES

DUM LOQUIMUR FUGERIT INVIDA

AETAS CARPE DIEM QUAM ININIME

CREDULA POSTERO

*While speaking so envious time has flown, seize
today, little trust the morrow.*

—A BOOK OF SUNDIAL MOTTOES

xperts would constrain today's gardeners
with the straitjacket of what they think
gardeners should or should not do with
plants, and rose care is the most constrained
and heritage-ridden of the entire plant kingdom. I
cannot begin to describe how many people have told me that
I cannot grow my roses as I do, that they will not grow when I
plant the bud unions that deeply. That, indeed, I should not mix
roses with other perennials in the garden because they don't
grow together. I have even had rose "experts" stand beside my
clay pots filled with wonderfully blooming roses and tell me
roses won't succeed in containers. I cannot begin to describe
their reactions to the 'Blaze' climbing rose in full blooming
glory—in a hanging basket. For some reason, rose growers prefer to believe their traditions before they believe their experience. Roses are like any other plant in the garden, to be grown
and enjoyed. Grow them; enjoy them in whatever manner you
can imagine because they are truly wonderful plants.

IF WE FREE OUR MINDS from the incubus of those usual teachings and practices, many beautiful things may be done with Roses for garden adornment.

—WILLIAM ROBINSON, *The English Flower Garden*

IT IS INSTRUCTIVE TO STUDY the influence of rose books upon the Rose as well as that of the Rose exhibitions, as they brought about an idea that the Rose was not a "decorative" plant in the language of recent days. In these books it was laid down that the Rose did not associate properly with other flowers, and it was therefore better to put it in a place by itself, and, though this false idea had less influence in the cottage garden, it did harm in all large gardens.

—WILLIAM ROBINSON, *The English Flower Garden*

ROSES AND SUNSHINE

One thing our garden experiments have confirmed is that the rose demands a minimum of six full hours of hot sunshine a day. Anything less than that and the plant will be smaller and produce smaller and fewer blossoms. More than six hours a day of sun is a bonus and the plant will respond in kind to the extra energy provided.

One of the great gardening myths of our time is that roses cannot be grown on sandy soils, that they require a heavy clay soil to succeed. I have grown roses on both sand- and clay-based soils, and I can safely report that if the water needs of the plant are met, sand is fine. On sandy soils, if you ignore the need for a constant source of water and food, flower production will plummet. This is not to say that roses like to have their roots sitting in water. Quite the contrary: What they appreciate is an evenly damp—not swampy or poorly drained—soil condition.

THE ROSE CAN BE NOURISHED for six to eight years without adding any manure to the surface, and after six, eight, or ten years most beds will probably require some change, or we may change our view as regards them.

— WILLIAM ROBINSON, *The English Flower Garden*

Feeding roses is an important job in the garden. Robinson would create a superbly rich bed by incorporating tons of manure to each bed on construction. He experienced, in that wonderful rose-growing environment of the British Isles, no degradation in bloom over six or more years. I find that regularly adding compost to the flower beds keeps the roses blooming well. I have never taken Robinson's approach and tried for a multiyear program. I have tried *not* feeding roses and the results were as expected—after the first year, the rose blossoms started to dwindle in numbers and the canes became thinner. By the fifth year, the roses were not worth keeping in the garden, being pale shadows of their well-fed cousins.

I do try to feed my tender roses at least once a week during the growing season. I say "try" to be honest. Quite often the slings and arrows of outrageous life will interfere with the enjoyment of the

ROSE TREE

garden. When this happens, I try to relax, apologize to the roses, and get on with gardening. This is not rocket science; it is gardening and meant to be a relaxing hobby, not a compulsion. Using a compost tea or liquid fish emulsion as regularly as possible keeps my roses strong and blooming all summer and provides enough food to enable them to survive our Canadian winters. I have found no proprietary liquid foods that work better than the emulsion or manure tea although there are a lot of them on the garden center shelves. Our spring garden program does not distinguish between roses and any other plant in the surrounding beds. All the plants get a ½ inch layer of compost to start off.

The mulch on my garden beds does several good things for the rose plants. The first thing is to create even soil moisture. This even state is perfect for roses — and most other plants — and allows me to cut back on my watering. The mulch stops the loss of moisture, saving water and the time it takes to apply it. Decomposing mulch provides organic matter to the soil, providing a food source for the microorganisms in the soil and eventually for the roses themselves, as well as insects. A common problem in our area is the earwig — *Forficula auricularia* — a garden scavenger whose food of choice is tender organic matter. In our garden, the earwigs stay hidden below the mulch, chomping away on the tender rotting mulch rather than coming up to feast on our flower buds and leaves. Mulch becomes an integral part of our insect control program with this pest; I would rather have them eating the mulch than my rose blossoms.

Mulch, at least the 3- to 4-inch layer I maintain, also keeps the majority of weeds at bay.

How to Plant Roses: Regular Versus Northern Planting

It is impossible to give any hard and fast rules for the culture of any plant which will apply in all cases. There may be suggestions herein offered which will not be applicable to all garden conditions.

— S. C. Hubbard, *Roses and Their Culture*

Hubbard (1926) has put his finger on one of the most frustrating points in gardening. There are few "hard and fast rules" that "apply in all cases." What works for me in my gardens may or may not work for you. There are no rules that work for all rose growers in all areas. If that is frustrating to rose experts and writers, I can only begin to imagine how it must be for a beginner looking for clear rules for growing this most glorious of flowers. That said, here are the main techniques I use for planting, wintering, and feeding roses.

In warmer climates, where winter is not a concern, rosebud unions are regularly planted 2 inches above the ground. In cooler climates, the bud union does well when planted 2 inches below the ground. In cold climates, there are a number of rose gardeners who plant the bud union 6 inches deep to protect it against winter. It is this last group—the author included—who have created controversy in the rose-growing world. Speaking only for myself, I have been growing tender roses and burying

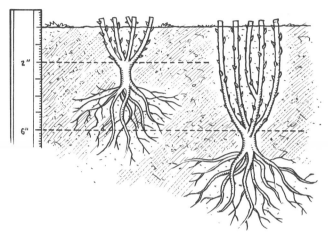

REGULAR PLANTING VERSUS NORTHERN PLANTING

the bud unions for the past ten years. It may not be successful
for other gardeners — I have had them stand beside my blooming roses and tell me the system would not work — but it does
work for me. See the illustration, above, for planting depths.

THEN COME ROSES, and we would strongly recommend that, in addition to the
newer "remontant" roses, the old roses and the old way of growing them
should not be quite forgotten.

　　— HENRY A. BRIGHT, *The English Flower Garden*

How to Feed for Production

THERE IS NO MORE MYSTERY about plant foods for roses than about soils. The
simple fact is that the queen of flowers is an ever-hungry organism which cannot help herself much to obtain the nourishment she needs.

　　— FREDERICK F. ROCKWELL, *The Home Gardener Handbook: Roses*

Our Mr. Rockwell—author of a significant number of gardening books—seems to have pegged the rose quite accurately when he describes her as "an ever-hungry organism." With the exception of William Robinson (1905), who tended to heavily manure his rose beds and then leave them alone, all our authors suggest feeding the rose quite heavily.

Animal manures, without doubt, furnish us excellent rose fertilizers. They not only supply actual plant foods but also keep the soil in such condition as to make the natural food supply more available.

— S. C. Hubbard, *Roses and Their Culture*

Hubbard (1926), a strong advocate of animal manure, suggested that "a two inch coat is about the right amount for cow or horse manures" while a "one inch covering of sheep manure is sufficient." He also promoted the use of manure tea. In fact, his is one of the clearest recipes for manure tea that I have seen in my book collection. He writes, "The liquids are made by using one half bushel of manure to one barrel of water. Allow to soak for twenty-four hours and use. It is best when made fresh each time. Five gallons of the solution should cover about thirty five square feet" (Hubbard 1926).

There is only one more aspect of feeding roses that should be addressed: timing. In the deep-planting system of growing roses, the roses are fed on a weekly basis, if possible, to keep them growing strongly throughout the season. With the root mass buried so deeply, you must liquid feed to supply the necessary nutrients. In my gardens, I try to feed once a week during the entire growing and flowering season right up until the garden freezes. In more traditional wintering systems — the soil-mounding and trenching system mentioned below — all plant food is withheld after the end of July. This gives the woody stalks a chance to harden up and ripen before winter. Hardened stalks are more likely to survive the winter than soft, overfed stems. I note that in the deep planting system, all canes are cut to the ground and discarded before winter sets in so their hardiness is not an issue — feeding the roots is the goal with this method.

DON'T FEED LATER THAN the first of August. To do so means unripened wood in the fall.

— S. C. HUBBARD, *Roses and Their Culture*

DEADHEADING/PRUNING

DEAD-HEADING THE ROSES ON A SUMMER evening is an occupation to carry us back into a calmer age and a different century. . . . There is no sound except the hoot of an owl, and the rhythmic snip-snip of our own secateurs, cutting the dead heads off, back to a new bud, to provoke new growth for the immediate future.

— VITA SACKVILLE-WEST, *More for Your Garden*

Only Vita Sackville-West could combine the romanticism of the earlier ages of gardening with the chore of deadheading spent flowers. Let me leave the images to her but remind our modern reader that deadheading roses is as important a task in the modern garden as it was a hundred years ago. Deadheading, removing the dead and spent flowers, is garden cleanliness. If

FRAGRANCE

WHAT IS THE LESSON these sweet flowers have for us? They tell us—if there were no other flowers to tell us—that a garden should be a living thing; its life not only fair in form and lovely in colour, but in its breath and essence coming from the Divine.

—WILLIAM ROBINSON, *The English Flower Garden*

There are countless references to the fragrance of roses throughout our literature and poetry yet it seems to me that the Irishman Robinson—a gardening bard himself—said it as well as it needs to be said. A garden is a living thing and one only has to take the time in the midst of our fast-paced world to stop and smell the roses to understand just how and where they came from. The fragrance of a rose is poetry and words can never, and need never, do it justice.

cleanliness is next to godliness—as my grandmother so often reminded me as a young boy—then keeping the garden clean and neat is a perfect evening's occupation. While my grandmother's words were in an often vain attempt to convince me to stay cleaner, keeping the old flowers pruned off leads to better and healthier plants and even more flowers.

Pruning stimulates plant growth. The more one prunes a young and vigorously growing rose, the more it will respond with new growth and flowers. The trick in all this activity is to channel the subsequent growth in the directions you desire.

THE TRUE GARDENER must be brutal, and imaginative for the future.

— VITA SACKVILLE-WEST, *More for Your Garden*

Sackville-West is quite right. Brutally cutting back the living shoots of any plant is quite difficult for beginning gardeners, yet it must be done if the plant is to respond with new blooms. It is the imagination that comes into play when the gardener, shears in hand, makes those fateful cuts. We do see, in our mind's eye, just where we want the new shoots to come from and how that will change the way the plant blooms and appears in our garden.

Make deadhead cuttings so that they follow these rules. Cut as far down the stem as it takes to find an outward-facing bud. Sometimes this cut will be a long way down — twelve to eighteen inches or more — but outward-facing buds grow out away from the central core of the plant and admit light and air to the center of the plant. Light and air circulation retard the growth of rose diseases. Pruning just above a bud encourages it to grow, whether it is inward or outward facing. Choose outward-facing buds whenever possible, but do not be too distraught if your only choice is an inward-facing one. Life will go on and the rose will continue to bloom.

Make your cut at a forty-five degree angle just above the bud, no more than a quarter-inch above the bud to be precise. Don't leave longer stubs because the stubs will die, leaving a dead section on the top of the cane. Dead stubs have several results. The first is an open invitation to fungal diseases to use the decaying stub as a source of food and further infection. The second is an

HOW TO PRUNE

unsightly appearance – a plant full of brown, dead, or dying wood is not attractive. The third is to loudly announce to the world that either a beginning or an uncaring gardener is in charge of this garden.

SEASONAL CARE

In mild climates, overwintering roses is a joy. One does absolutely nothing beyond basic fall pruning and the plant survives. For a gardener living in a mostly USDA Zone 4 garden, where winter temperatures can occasionally plunge to –40° F for a week or more, having a mild rose-growing climate sounds like something just this side of paradise. Many of my rose-growing friends plant in the traditional manner for cool climates; that is, they put the bud union down 2 inches below the soil line. This means in the winter they have several options. They can do nothing and take their chances, hoping the plant will survive; they can employ dif-

ferent systems of mulching; or they can tip the plant over and
bury it in the soil.

We will not even discuss the do-nothing option. It is the last
bastion of hope for the terminally time-challenged among us.
These are the gardeners who haunt the cut-rate discount shelves
looking for bargains every spring because they treat their roses
as annual flowers.

THE SIMPLEST AND most effective form of protection for garden or bush roses
is hilling up the soil about the plants.
— FREDERICK F. ROCKWELL, *The Home Gardener Handbook: Roses*

The simplest overwintering system is hilling with soil.
Excavate soil from another part of the garden and mound it
up over the canes until it resembles something created by
Cheops or Rameses. The most effective height of the mound is
18 to 24 inches tall. The canes are normally cut back to 18 to
24 inches themselves so they just stick out over the top of
the mound. For the most part, covering roses with deep mounds
of soil works very well. Some gardeners, not content with only
a soil mound, add piles of leaves or cover the entire bed with
an insulating plastic foam frost cover. Others make styrofoam-
lined boxes for their roses, giving each one a personal home for
the winter months. Whatever system a gardener may choose, the
objective is to create as frost-free an environment as possible
to overwinter the rose. The deeper the better is the key for
protection by mulch.

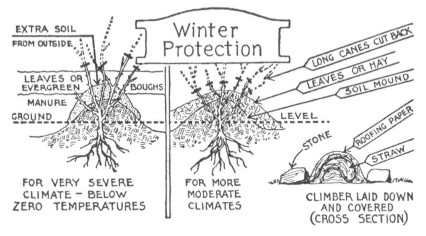

WINTER PROTECTION

In the spring, as soon as the soil and mulch start to thaw they are removed; the mulch to the compost pile, the soil to its original location. The canes are cut back to 12 to 18 inches and if all has gone according to plan, buds will begin to swell within a few weeks. If things have not gone well, the rose will be dead. Sometimes the top of the rose has died, yet the rootstock has not and will send long shoots up in an attempt to gather strength. These shoots are easy to recognize because they come from below the bud union. They are not worth growing. Dig out the rose and discard it.

There are also gardeners who tip their roses over in the fall. This means they dig a trench as long and wide as the plant is tall. The rose is bundled up with twine or rope, the roots loosened

MANURE

SOIL FROM
TRENCH

CANES

HUBBARD SYSTEM OF ROSE OVERWINTERING

with digging forks (shovels cut the roots) and then the rose is "tipped" or "trenched" over to lie down in the eight- to twelve-inch-deep trench. The soil from the excavation is piled back over the trench and 6 to 12 inches of leaves are used as an insulation layer over the top of the trench. This is an excellent method of overwintering roses but quite labor intensive. Hubbard (1926) did not approve of digging trenches or burying roses. He wrote,

> The term 'bury' as used here does not mean that a trench should be dug. On the contrary, avoid any depression in which water may stand. Water around the canes means dead wood in the spring. Lay the bundles of canes straight out upon the ground and pin them down with wires or wooden pegs. If on a sloping site, lay the tips lower than the crown of the plant, thereby eliminating any chance of water

collecting at the base. Now remove the soil from both sides of the bundles and use it in covering. This leaves the canes on a ridge of ground so that the water may drain off on either side. Use plenty of soil around the crown. After the soil is solidly frozen, a covering of manure eight to ten inches deep is given. This method has proved one hundred percent efficient (Hubbard 1926).

While it might be 100 percent efficient, it still sounds like a lot of work to me.

Gardeners who use the deep planting system do nothing for the winter except cut the rose canes down to the ground and remove the debris. The roses are left to resprout from the underground canes the following spring, as if they were a herbaceous perennial plant. This is a good wintering technique for most roses, although to be successful with this system, you *must* follow the section on feeding as well. Simply deep planting and then ignoring the rose will not produce a satisfactory plant or a significant number of blossoms. To be fair about it, none of the classic authors considered using this system and it sparks considerable debate among today's experts.

Pests and Disease

Most insect pests that bother roses are also pests of other plants in the garden and have been thoroughly discussed in other sections of this book. (See Chapter 6 for discussions on insect damage.) However, Mrs. Loudon had a particular aversion to aphids that deserves mentioning here: "But of all the insects that infest the rose, the most destructive are the aphids. These little green flies cover the tender leaves and buds of the young shoots in myriads, and are extremely difficult to destroy, without spoiling the appearance of the shoots that have been attacked by them. Tobacco water is an excellent remedy, if not too strong. It should be made by steeping half-a-pound of the best tobacco in a gallon of hot water; and as soon as the infusion has become cold, the shoots should be dipped in it, and suffered to remain a few seconds, after which they should be immediately washed in clean water before they are suffered to dry" (Loudon [1843] 1851).

What I haven't covered are the diseases that are either specific to or particularly damaging to roses. There are two major diseases of roses that repeatedly crop up in the literature: powdery mildew and black spot.

Powdery mildew is best described by Hubbard (1926): "The first signs of the disease are grayish white spots on the young leaves and shoots. Later the spots have a white powdery appearance, while still later this powdery covering disappears leaving dark colored areas. The buds, young shoots and leaves are curled and stunted." As you might imagine, if the older leaves are left spotted and dark while the younger foliage and shoots are misshapen, the plant's growth and flower production will be severely reduced. There are several things the rose grower can do to control powdery mildew. They start with selecting varieties that are resistant to the disease, if possible. Beginning gardeners should note that resistance does not mean that the rose is

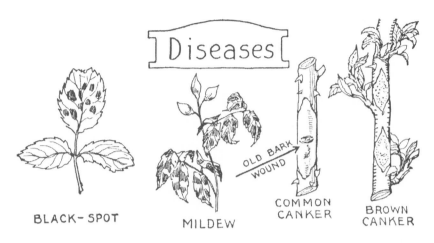

Diseases

BLACK-SPOT   MILDEW   OLD BARK WOUND   COMMON CANKER   BROWN CANKER

DISEASES OF THE ROSE

immune to the problem. Resistance simply means that it is *less likely* to get mildew or will get it only in wet seasons or conditions where it is particularly virulent.

THE MOST EFFECTIVE REMEDY for powdery mildew is to dust the infected plants with a mixture of very finely ground sulphur 90 parts, and arsenate of lead 10 parts.

— S. C. HUBBARD, *Roses and Their Culture*

Toxic arsenate of lead *is not recommended* for gardening application, but sulfur is still very much recommended as a control for powdery mildew. Use a liquid lime-sulfur spray — available at most garden centers — and apply it as directed on the label. Dusting with powdered sulfur is also suggested by modern authors; it controls powdery mildew by creating an acid condition on the leaf surface that kills mildew spores.

IT HAS RECENTLY BEEN PROVED that rose plants growing in soil well supplied with potash were almost immune from mildew.

—S. C. HUBBARD, *Roses and Their Culture*

While I do not know about adding potash to control mildew, I do know that using baking soda is a good preventative and cure. Mix two tablespoons to a gallon of warm water and spray this onto the leaves both to stop powdery mildew and retard its establishment. Adding a dash of soap into the mix before spraying will assist the soda in spreading and sticking to the leaf surface. Baking soda can be quite caustic, so spray a small leaf test area and wait twenty-four hours to evaluate if there is any leaf "burning" or damage before spraying the entire plant. I always test each plant and recommend you do so as well, because variations in leaf thickness and small deviations in mixing amounts of the soda and water create different effects on the leaves.

BLACK SPOT IS undoubtedly the most destructive disease of the rose.

—S. C. HUBBARD, *Roses and Their Culture*

"Black spot is easily recognized by the appearance, in late spring or early summer, of irregular circular spots on the upper surface of the leaves, and almost invariably on the lower leaves of the plant first. As the spots grow, they become more irregular and darker in color; new ones appear and the leaf becomes yellow and will fall at a touch" (Rockwell 1930). This description

is as good as it need be for today's gardener. The spots do start on the bottom and the leaves eventually drop at touch or of their own accord.

Black spot is one of those diseases that is almost as common as rose growing. If you have roses, you have black spot. It is most likely to be severe in damp or prolonged wet weather when the bacteria responsible is kept damp. Growing roses in morning shade, when the dew is allowed to stay on the leaves for prolonged periods, will also contribute to the establishment of black spot.

Control of black spot demands attention to several different details. First you must understand that once black spot is established on a leaf, it is impossible to spray it and kill the bacteria, which is between the leaf surfaces rather than sitting on top. This means that our first step is a preventative program to slow down black spot's establishment. Control begins with sanitation. Clean up all leaf debris in the fall; the bacteria will easily over-winter on infected leaves so removing them from the garden to the landfill eliminates that source of infestation. The second step in the fall is to spray all overwintering canes with a dormant oil and lime-sulfur spray. (Dormant oil is a light, horticultural oil that is sprayed onto a plant while it's dormant to smother pest eggs and reduce disease.) Spores overwinter in the cracks of cane wood; a spray will kill them. It is a good idea to respray the dormant oil again first thing in the spring, immediately after the winter mulch has been removed, to catch any surviving bacteria. Summer control involves removing any leaves that are infected and taking them from the garden. Start a preventative spray program in the spring if you had a problem the previous summer. Spray lime-sulfur one week and baking soda the next; alternating these sprays a week apart all summer will provide very good preventative control.

When black spot rears its head in the summer, prune off infected leaves as soon as you see them. Start spraying weekly and repeat after every rain. These recommendations may not eliminate black spot from the garden but they will reduce it to a manageable level.

CHAPTER SIX

CONTAINER GROWING

L'HEURE PASSE, L'AMITIE RESTE

The hour passes, friendship stays.

—A BOOK OF SUNDIAL MOTTOES

Many plants can be successfully grown in a container. In our gardens, I grow a wide range of roses, herbaceous perennials, alpines, water garden plants, evergreens, and yes, even annuals in containers. My garden would be the poorer if it were constrained to the traditional annual-in-a-bucket look. I also believe that gardeners who restrict their plant choice to those plants advocated by the horticultural industry as container plants cheapen their own gardening experience. To me, one part of gardening is learning to be adventurous, to be bold with the use of plants. To raise the plant you like in the place you want to enjoy it is the ultimate growing experience. Container gardening allows you to enjoy any plant in almost any location.

PROBABLY NO OTHER OCCUPATION or amusement is more innocent in itself, or more devoid of injury or annoyance to others, than the cultivation of flowers.
— JULIUS HEINRICH, *The Window Flower Garden*

There are four primary factors to be considered when growing container plants: the container itself, the appropriate soil for the plant, feeding the plant, and providing adequate water. Each of these factors is considered below.

SEVERAL PEOPLE HAVE WRITTEN to ask me what to do about their sink-gardens during the winter. I couldn't care more.
— VITA SACKVILLE-WEST, *More for Your Garden*

WHERE THE ARCHITECTURE of a house is dull and featureless, or the surroundings leave much to be desired, the use of window boxes not only brings cheer to the rooms behind, but imparts an air of gaiety to the whole street.
— FRANCES PERRY, *The Woman Gardener*

CONTAINERS

The choice of container is as important in the garden as the choice of plant to fill it. These initial choices set the tone for the rest of the adventure. A pair of old rubber boots can indeed be used to hold geraniums and petunias, and this choice of container sends an entirely different design message than a hot-fired Italian clay pot filled with the same plants. The first time a tipped-over barrel is filled with flowers to make it appear as if the flowers were spilling out over the lawn, it is cute. An entire street of such barrels resembles a gaudy theme park more than a gardening neighborhood. The easiest way to determine your personal style is to spend a winter examining the pictures of container gardens in magazines and books. Keep a record of the containers that particularly appeal to your sense of gardening style and copy those designs and pots in your own garden. Imitation *is* the sincerest form of flattery.

Clay Pots

FLOWER POTS ARE of many different kinds, but the common red earthen-ware are decidedly the best, because they are the most porous, and consequently do not retain the moisture so as to be injurious to the plants they contain.

—JANE LOUDON, *Gardening for Ladies and Companion to the Flower Garden*

Clay pots are the best for growing plants. I say this after twenty years in the nursery business and twenty years of growing a wide variety of plants in every kind of container in the industry. To be sure, clay has its drawbacks, but its ability to support plant life is not one of them. Clay is heavy, it breaks if dropped, and is more expensive than plastic. These are the drawbacks to clay cited by other gardeners, but these are more than compensated for in my mind by the superior growth conditions clay provides. I was delighted when I obtained Julius Heinrich's book (1911) on container gardening and found he shared my opinion. In a discussion of pots he wrote, "After years of trial and experience, I find that the best pots in which to grow plants are the common clay pots."

Clay pots breathe. Moisture moves through the sidewalls as well as downward through the soil. This moisture on the sidewalls evaporates during hot summer days, providing a potential cooling effect to the soil and plant roots that plastic pots do not duplicate. Clay is heavier than other pot materials, but this is to its advantage during summer windstorms. It does not tip over as readily, leaving crushed plants and ruined blossoms scattered in its wake. I like the solidity that clay brings to the garden, and while I confess that the look of clay has been duplicated by plastic pots, the more important ability to breathe has not. And clay, unlike plastic, will not break down in sunlight and can, with careful handling, last for many years in the garden.

To place a beautiful vase in a distant part of the grounds, where there is no direct allusion to art, and where it is accompanied only by natural objects, as the overhanging trees and the sloping turf, is in a measure doing violence to our reason or taste, by bringing two objects so strongly contrasted, in direct union.

— Andrew J. Downing, *Landscape Gardening*

If you are going to use clay pots, purchase the high or hot-fired clay. They will not "spall" — or flake off pieces of their sides—in the garden during the winter months. I have some of these good pots in my garden that are twenty years old, while the cheaper clay pots only last a few years before they must be tossed into the local landfill. The more expensive high-temperature-fired pots can even be left outside over the winter in our Zone 4 garden without damage.

Plastic Pots

As a nurseryman, I have grown more plants in plastic pots than any other kind and they do have advantages. All forms of plastic pots on the market hold water better than similarly sized clay pots. This is one reason the nursery trade uses plastic: A plant growing in a plastic pot will require less frequent watering than one grown in clay. The plastic does not sweat—or cool down the plant—through the sidewalls. The second reason the nursery trade moved to plastic was that it is significantly lighter than clay. If a plant has to be moved, a light plastic pot makes the task that much easier. Plastic is also cheaper than clay, and this can be a significant difference when you need more than a few pots. Plastic does not break as easily as clay, but it does break down in the sunlight. After a few years, cheap plastic pots become so much plastic dust in the garden.

In placing plants on shelves, stands, tables, etc., always have a saucer under the pot, but never allow it to get full of water, else the soil will get too wet, and cause the roots to rot.

—Julius Heinrich, *The Window Flower Garden*

Both the large clay and plastic pots can have their drainage holes sealed to make them watertight. I use a hot-glue gun for this purpose and then use the watertight pots for growing my water lilies and bog plants.

Wooden Pots

Wooden tubs or window boxes also grow a good plant. In our area, the whiskey barrel is the preferred container for dockside planting. It is heavy enough that it cannot be blown around or "borrowed" by passersby; it is large enough that it survives a week or more without watering; and it looks good when painted and maintained. There are even liners now available in garden centers that will turn these half barrels into small water gardens.

Next to the clay pot, a wooden box or tub is best.

—Julius Heinrich, *The Window Flower Garden*

Many friends and customers have complained about their window boxes after a few years of gardening. There are two methods to retard rotting that have worked well for me. The first and best solution is to line the window box. A metal liner is the optimum solution but—since I never seemed able to afford such luxury—I make my wooden boxes the right size so that the paper-fiber boxes available at garden centers drop right inside. Two fiber window boxes drop into the wooden liner, and the wooden-box look is complete without the problem of rotting wood.

Window boxes are also much used; they can be made of plain boards or carved wood. These boxes are very ornamental, and are excellent for holding pots of plants, which is much better than planting them in the soil, as when a plant stops blooming it can easily be replaced with another. The vacant spaces are to be filled with moss.

—Julius Heinrich, *The Window Flower Garden*

Heinrich (1911) also suggested simply placing the potted plants into the wooden boxes without using soil in the wooden box. If you pack peat moss around the potted plants to help hold them upright and act as a moisture reserve, the plants will thrive for the summer. This is an excellent technique for summering houseplants outdoors. For years I have held many of my greenhouse stock plants in large containers constructed of railroad ties and packed with wet peat. While on a somewhat larger scale than the average homeowner would require, the technique is the same and the results, as measured by plant growth and summer bloom, are excellent. The plants grow well all summer, and in the fall are quite content to move back indoors.

Concrete/Foam Pots

Concrete tubs and the newer foam pots act very much like plastic pots in the way they grow plants. The obvious advantage of the foam pots is their extreme lightness, which makes them easy to move in the garden. If you are the kind of gardener who rearranges plants as you would furniture, this lack of weight may be to your advantage. Concrete, on the other hand, is of a more permanent nature. The foam has not been on the market long enough to evaluate how it degrades in sunlight, but because it is impermeable, it will act exactly like plastic for watering. Concrete, although it does sweat if kept full of water, acts more like plastic than clay for holding water, and, if properly made, it will not degrade in the sunlight.

BESIDES THE COMMON FLOWER-POTS, there are double pots, one of which has been sent me by Capt. Mangles, which are very useful for balconies, as the roots of the plants are very apt to be injured, by the outside of the pot in which they grow being dried by the wind, or heated by the sun. When double pots are used, the interstice between the pots should be stuffed with moss kept moist.

— JANE LOUDON, *Gardening for Ladies and Companion to the Flower Garden*

SOILS

YET WHAT IS THE HISTORY of millions of plants grown for the dwelling-houses of all classes? They are placed where they are intended to live. They are watered day after day to excess; the water runs into the saucer in which the pot is placed, and there the poor things stand till their roots rot; they get worse by degrees, until they can stand it no longer. The leaves drop or dry

A CROCK OF POTTING SOIL

THE BEST SOIL for plants in pots is generally peat mixed with vegetable mould and sand; and the pots should be filled nearly a quarter of their depth with little bits of broken pots, called potsherds, so to ensure complete drainage.

—JANE LOUDON, *Gardening for Ladies and Companion to the Flower Garden*

ELASTIC PLANT
SPRINKLER

One old gardening practice that should be eliminated is putting old potsherds or gravel or some other material at the bottom of the pot, as Mrs. Loudon suggests, "so to ensure complete drainage." In theory, this sounds good, but in practice, it does not work. Water, moving downward through containers, slows down every time it hits a different layer of material. This means that regardless of whether the water is moving from soil to potsherds or from potsherds to soil, the physics of water movement will create a damp layer at the interchange between the two different materials. The potsherds do not help water drain more quickly; they slow it down. To ensure complete and proper drainage, fill the container with the same soil from top to bottom.

IN PLANTING BULBS in pots, the same primary rules of drainage should be observed. This is effected by filling the pots with about an inch of broken potsherds, or "crocks," and then filling up with prepared soil. Small bits of charcoal, about the size of a hazel-nut, make a very good drainage, and contribute to heighten the brilliancy of the flowers.

—EDWARD SPRAGUE RAND, JR., *Bulbs: A Treatise on Hardy and Tender Bulbs and Perennials* upon the stems, and the good people think what pity it is plants will not live in their locality.

—Thomas Mawe and John Abercrombie, *The Complete Gardener*

No other factor is as important to success in container gardening as is the soil in the container. With the proper soil, any plant can be grown in a pot; with the wrong soil, failure is guaranteed. I can say without reservation that the best soil for general growing of annuals or nonspecialized perennials is one of the artificial soil mixes composed of peat moss and perlite. While there are other ingredients to these mixes, such as wetting agents and sometimes compost, the two main components will allow the gardener to grow just about any plant to be found in a garden center with the exception of alpines and water-garden plants. Do I expect the old-time garden authors or more modern garden authorities to agree wholeheartedly with me on this? Not likely. Soil is one of those things that gardeners love to disagree over, and there are almost as many customized soil mixes as there are specialized gardeners. I can only tell you that the artificial mixes work very well for me and they are readily available in most garden centers.

JOHN INNES COMPOST

2 parts by bulk medium loam

1 parts by bulk leaf or peat

1 parts by bulk coarse sand

to every bushel of the above mix add

1.5 ozs. of superphosphate

.75 ozs. of limestone

—Frances Perry, *The Woman Gardener*

For alpine plants, I mix the artificial soil fifty-fifty with either sand or turface to give a faster-draining soil. Quick drainage is of the utmost importance to many alpines, which will die if left sitting in damp soils. To better understand the reasoning behind this, simply ask yourself when you ever saw a mountaintop with excellent soil. Most alpine settings have gritty, gravelly soils and this is the kind of soil I use in containers reserved for alpines. My water plants get a heavier soil; the best topsoil I can find with no peat moss or other light additives included. I use this heavier, but extremely fertile, soil in all containers for bog plants or water lilies. I generally dig my own topsoil from a corner of the garden, but if you must purchase your topsoil ensure that it is free of peat moss. Adding peat moss, and sometimes composted manure, is a favorite garden center practice to ensure a good-looking soil. The composted manure is a fine addition to the water garden soil (see Chapter 7 for water garden soils) but the lighter, floating peat moss is not welcome in my ponds.

If the soil requirements of the plant demand excellent drainage, then add grit of some kind to the artificial soil mix until the soil drains at the required speed. In the old literature, authors such as Rand (1866) have sometimes recommended adding charcoal to the soil for various reasons. We do know that charcoal absorbs a wide variety of toxic compounds, so perhaps there is good reason to add it to our soil mixes. If you want to add it, blend it into the soil mix rather than leaving it as a separate layer, which will retard the drainage of water through the pot.

I can hear the question reverberating now from more than one reader. What about garden soil in containers? Can I use topsoil for my containerized plants? With the exception of water and bog plants and some rare alpine plants (see above), my experience is that using garden soil in containers creates more problems than it is worth. The major reason to avoid garden soil is that it compacts terribly under the conditions found in containers. Adding several inches of water to a container in a single watering creates compaction; it forces the soil particles to jam together and eliminates air spaces. Doing this repeatedly, as we have to do with our smaller containers, increases the problem. The air spaces created by perlite in artificial container soil stop compaction, allowing tender roots to receive their needed oxygen and grow. Without this necessary air space (20 percent by volume at a minimum), roots grow badly and water drains slowly. With compacted soil and poor drainage, inadequate plant growth is guaranteed. That is the long way of recommending that, old-time authors notwithstanding, you should avoid real soil in the average plant container.

FEEDING CONTAINER PLANTS

PLANTS REQUIRE FRESH AIR; therefore give it to them on every fine sunny and warm day. . . . This airing gives the plants a healthy and vigorous growth, also a good color, while those that have no fresh air, although they have all the other care possible, will still be of slender, soft growth, not unlike many of the children raised in our fashionable homes.

—JULIUS HEINRICH, *The Window Flower Garden*

For the most part, container plants are the most underfed plants in our gardens. We forget that nitrogen, the main engine of plant growth, is water-soluble. Every time we water our plants, we dissolve nitrogen and take it out of the bottom of the pots along with the drainage water. If we do not replace it at the top of the containers, then very shortly none is available to feed the plants. We wonder why they are not performing as well as the neighbors' or as well as at the garden center.

EXPERIENCE HAS DEMONSTRATED that good, well-rotted cow manure is, in all cases, the best for house-plants. Water can be placed on the manure, and the liquid thus obtained can be used to good advantage in watering the plants.

—JULIUS HEINRICH, *The Window Flower Garden*

Containerized plants can be fed on an ongoing basis either with a liquid plant food or with one of the long-term, slow-release fertilizers. In my garden, particularly with greedy-feeding plants such as roses, I use several tablespoons of slow-release pellets scattered over the surface of a 14- or 16-inch pot, and then I liquid-feed the plant on a weekly basis as well. The slow-release feed gives the plant baseline nutrition so that it will continue growing but my liquid feeding seems to provide extra strength to the blossoms. Unlike Heinrich (1911), who prefers a compost or manure tea for his container plants, I like a liquid fish emulsion. While the fish emulsion is a bit, well . . . fishy-smelling, it provides many of the trace nutrients an artificial soil lacks. Sometimes, particularly with ailing plants, the overnight response to the fish emulsion is nothing short of sensational. Fish emulsion is available at most garden centers and, while I particularly recommend it for roses, it works well on any plant in a container. To prevent sounding too enthusiastic about the fish emulsion, I hasten to add that any liquid plant food — from houseplant food to specialized container food — will grow an excellent summer-flowering container. Nitrogen is nitrogen and how you add it to your container is irrelevant. It is simply important that you do.

[PLANT FOOD] SHOULD BE APPLIED at evenings, upon the soil in the pot, and not upon the foliage, which should not be spattered with the solution.
— JULIUS HEINRICH, *The Window Flower Garden*

Heinrich (1911) would have us take extra care in the application of his liquid manure to plants, doing the task in the evening as well as avoiding splashing the leaves. I can understand his reluctance to touch the leaves of plants; even though I have never burned a plant leaf with manure tea, it may be possible. The residue on the plant leaf may also hold its proprietary fragrance for a longer time, definitely something to avoid if possible, especially if the plant is close to windows or doorways. Watering or feeding outdoor container plants in the evening is, in my opinion and contrary to much of the garden literature, almost irrelevant when it comes to disease control. Water and feed outdoor containers whenever you have the time and inclination. This is not true of indoor containerized plants. You should water them in the morning so the excess moisture has a chance to evaporate and leave the plant canopy dry by evening.

I confess I am not sure why outdoor plants do not resent having their leaves wet all night as indoor plants do, but I have observed this on more than one occasion in my gardens, greenhouses, and nursery. Outdoor plants are much more resilient than their indoor cousins and, as long as they *are* watered and fed regularly and properly, they will thrive. Having said that, given the choice of a morning or evening watering, choose the morning since it will leave the plant canopy dry by evening; there is no sense in tempting the fates.

NOTHING IS WORSE than the small quantities of water, which probably reaches an inch down, and all the fibres below that remain dry and perish; the result of which is that leaves turn yellow, and dry on, or fall off, as the case may be.

—THOMAS MAWE AND JOHN ABERCROMBIE, *The Complete Gardener*

WATERING

There is a very simple rule when it comes to watering container plants: Always water so that at least 15 to 20 percent of the water poured in the top comes out the bottom. Having done this, do not water again until the surface of the soil is just dry to the touch. This system of watering ensures that the entire soil ball is wet so tender young roots do not go begging for moisture. If the soil ball is wet right to the bottom of the pot, the roots, too, will grow to the bottom of the pot. Deeply rooted plants are invariably healthier and better able to resist stress than are more shallowly rooted ones. A thorough watering also ensures that any excess fertilizer is always being moved to the bottom and right out of the pot so as not to damage the tender young feeder roots.

ANOTHER REASON WHY plants kept in rooms are generally unhealthy, is, that they are watered in a very irregular manner.

— JANE LOUDON, *Gardening for Ladies and Companion to the Flower Garden*

Should the artificial soil mix dry right out, it will pull away from the sides of the pot as it shrinks. This will allow the water to run quickly and easily down between the pot wall and the soil ball, not doing any good to the plant in the process. The remedy for shrinking soil is to set the pot in a tub or pail of water for at least an hour to allow the soil ball to absorb all the water it can handle and expand again. If the container is too large to move into a tub, very slow and often repeated waterings will accomplish the same thing. I have often had to trickle water over some of the larger containers three or four times, with a half hour between waterings, to convince them to rehydrate and soak up moisture.

The secret to watering containers, whether they be inside or outside potted plants, is to learn restraint. If you touch the soil and your finger comes away damp, then do not add more water. Too much water will kill a plant almost as fast as will too little.

PESTS

Most pests that bother plants in outdoor containers come under the heading of either aphids or spider mites. Throw in the odd caterpillar, mealybug, or scale and the cast of common pests is fully assembled.

While Mrs. Loudon has often been accused of spreading inaccurate gardening practices, in this she had a good point. Frequent misting does indeed knock back both aphids and spider mites. If aphids are hosed off a plant with a sharp spray, these same aphids do not climb back onto the plant. More may, and likely will, hatch from survivors but repeated and forceful sprayings will easily keep the aphid population under control. Spider mites do not seem to be as easily affected by a sharp spray of water, but they do not like repeated mistings since their foraging and breeding seem to be affected by the water. In my experience, this is more a preventative insect control than a remedy for a mite infestation. To knock back mite problems, I rely on insecticidal soap sprays. Soap, mixed at one part soap to forty parts water does an admirable job of killing mites and other soft-bodied insects (such as aphids).

WASHING WITH A SYRINGE, and abundance of water, is, however, probably a better mode; as it has been often observed that neither the green fly nor the red spider will ever infest a plant that is frequently syringed.

— JANE LOUDON, *Gardening for Ladies and Companion to the Flower Garden*

BRASS SYRINGE

THE MEALY BUG is easily seen and found by the white flowery or mealy appearance this insect presents when fully developed. Picking out the bugs with a small pointed piece of stick is about the best and safest method of keeping down these white, but objectionable and undesirable pests.

— LINUS WOOLVERTON, ED., *The Canadian Horticulturalist*

Mealybugs and scale are somewhat harder to kill with soap because they have protective outer coats that repel the soap sprays. Some gardeners add one part rubbing alcohol to the soap spray to help the soap penetrate the waxy surface. Others take a simpler approach and simply rub the offending insect with a toothbrush dipped in the soap solution. A sharp-pointed stick is as simple a solution as can be found for mealybugs and works quite nicely if time is of no concern. While *The Canadian Horticulturalist* may have recommended whale oil soap — a product that is in short supply today — its advice to move scale before spraying is quite good and effective.

THE BEST REMEDY is to wash off the scale with a weak solution of whale oil soap and water. It used to be a common saying amongst gardeners in my apprenticeship days that "to move the scale was to kill it," so that friction sufficient to move the scale is desirable, as well as the application of the solution as mentioned.

— LINUS WOOLVERTON, ED., *The Canadian Horticulturalist*

Whatever remedy you choose against common garden pests — whether water sprays, soaping, or even hand-picking the odd caterpillar — remember the advice of Linus Woolverton (1901), editor of *The Canadian Horticulturalist*: "Too often the application of preventatives and remedies is neglected until the plants are infested with insects, when severe measures have to be taken, and strong solutions used, that will perhaps kill the plant before it removes the pest." This remains true to this day. It is far better to control pests when they are newly established rather than when they are firmly entrenched on the plant. To avoid that, the gardener needs discerning and constant attention. Some things never change.

DISEASES

Most diseases of container plants fall into the root rot, mildew, or leaf spot fungus categories. Root rot is primarily caused by overwatering; when combined with cool temperatures, overwatering is an invitation to a variety of rot-type problems. The simplest solution is to water as recommended above and to move outdoor container plants inside for any short periods of cool temperatures. Other environmentally sound controls include the use of a garlic drench to combat existing problems. (See pages 74–75 for the recipe for garlic chunks.)

Mildews and leaf spot fungus problems are easily treated with lime-sulfur mixes, available at garden centers, or a mix of two tablespoons of baking soda in a gallon of warm water. The baking soda might burn tender leaves, such as impatiens, so it is important to test a few leaves first and dilute the concentration of baking soda by adding extra water if burning occurs. The classic method is to spray the test leaves and wait twenty-four hours to assess any damage. Both of these, the lime-sulfur spray and baking soda, will need to be repeated weekly or after rains have washed the leaves. As with pests, constant and immediate attention is needed to stop diseases before they become established.

Chapter Seven

Water Gardening

*Let others tell of storms and showers, I'll only count
your sunny hours.*

—A Book of Sundial Mottoes

Water gardening is fun. I will let other authors wax
poetic about the serenity of the still water and the
amazing way it draws creatures in its mimicry of
natural settings. I like the rippling water, the
splashing fish, and the gorgeous plants. The frogs in
the lilies make me smile. It is fun, and that is enough
reason for any garden.

Water gardening is easy gardening. There
are only a few basic rules—all found in this chapter—for success. It is not like alpine gardening, in which each
tiny plant demands a special rock crevice and soil mix. Water
plants like water, and, luckily, water comes in one standard variety—wet. Fill something with water, plonk in some plants,
and the water garden is born. Once you learn how to control
the algae, get huge blossoms on the lilies, and overwinter the
plants, the fun begins.

Lest the tyro may have the impression that pond-keeping is a troublesome
business, let me say at the outset that it is quite the reverse. When once a
pond has been established on natural principles, it needs practically no attention save, perhaps, the periodical pruning of plants which may spread so

rapidly as to hamper the movement of the fishes — and I shall show that both fishes and purely aquatic plants are necessary.

— A. E. HODGE, *Garden Ponds and Pools*

HOW TO PLANT

AT NO TIME allow the plants to be exposed to the drying action of the sun or air, as they will then very soon wilt and be seriously damaged, indeed, in many cases such drying, while waiting for the pond to fill up would be fatal.

— WILLIAM TRICKER, *The Water Garden*

Well, plonking in the plants is as close to the reality of the water garden as I can begin to describe. The illustration (opposite) shows how to plant a hardy water lily. The important point to remember is not to plant the crown below the surface of the soil. Sink the rest of the tuber in the soil and weigh it down with some rocks until it has established roots. Each tuber is angled slightly differently. Some may require horizontal planting and others may require angled planting to ensure the tuber is buried but the crown is above the soil line.

THE SEASON FOR PLANTING will vary according to locality and section, but it may be considered perfectly safe to plant all hardy Nymphaeas and other aquatics (except Nelumbians) as soon as vegetation is assured.

— WILLIAM TRICKER, *The Water Garden*

I am often asked about the timing for planting hardy water lilies. Water garden nursery workers wear wet suits when they start their spring work the day after the ice has left their ponds,

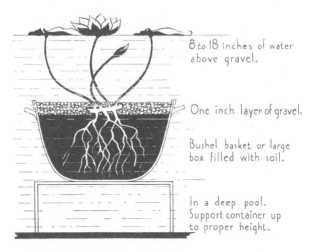

8 to 18 inches of water above gravel.

One inch layer of gravel.

Bushel basket or large box filled with soil.

In a deep pool. Support container up to proper height.

THE WATER LILY PLANTED IN AN AVERAGE POND

but this dedication is not something I aspire to. The hardy lilies do not seem to mind any water temperature — in nature, the water above them is often frozen solid so any temperature above "solid ice" is an improvement from their point of view.

In this sense, they are like any other plant. If forced to grow in a warmer area such as a greenhouse, they should be properly acclimatized. Otherwise, delay purchasing and planting lilies until the outside temperatures rise up to those of the protected environment. Moving from warm to cold water is no better for the lily than it is for the gardener.

THE PLANTING OF the hardy water lilies can be done at any time from the start of growth in the Spring, generally about April first, up to the last week of August. While plants set out before or after these dates may do all right, there

is a certain amount of danger of losing the roots by a late spring or an early
cold fall, retarding the growth.

—PETER BISSET, *The Book of Water Gardening*

Bisset has good advice when he outlines his planting dates.
In my own gardens, I rarely move or divide a plant after finishing
the spring work. While summer planting results are acceptable,
fall planting has not been very successful for me so I avoid it with
hardy water lily plants.

Tender tropical lilies demand warm water. They arrive from
the growers as small tubers resembling bulbs, which are planted
2 to 3 inches deep into the pond. Planting and installing them in
water that is less than 70°F is an invitation to stunted growth and
possibly death, yet many gardeners continue to rush the season
with their tropical plants. In my Zone 4 gardens, the tropicals do
not normally go outside until the first or second week of June.

THE TENDER OR TROPICAL water lilies should not be planted until settled warm
weather arrives, or until the temperature of the water reaches nearly 70°F.

—PETER BISSET, *The Book of Water Gardening*

One question that I hear quite regularly in the nursery is
whether moving a plant from the nursery or water garden to a
deeper water garden would hurt the leaves. Would the plant
adjust to the different water levels? It is easy to take the words of
Tricker (1897), from his book *The Water Garden*: "It is immaterial
whether or not the water be deeper than that in which the plants
have been growing previously; the plant will adjust itself to the
new quarters, and in an incredibly short space of time the leaves

will be floating on the surface of the water, even if submerged two feet at the time of planting."

How Deep the Pond?

The depth of the pond is a personal preference and each author has his or her own experience to draw from. My experience in Zone 4 winters says that if the lilies and fish are to overwinter in the pond, then some sections should be at least 4 feet deep. The water at this depth will not freeze solid and fish and plants will overwinter comfortably.

THE POND SHOULD BE EXCAVATED to a depth of two feet six inches. This will allow of four inches of clay on the bottom, eight inches of soil, and one foot six inches of water.

— PETER BISSET, *The Book of Water Gardening*

Bisset recommends "two feet six inches" of excavation to build a pond, but then he is going to fill a foot of that back up with clay and soil for the lilies. This will leave him with only "one foot six inches of water" for the lilies, which is a perfect amount of water to have over the lily crowns. The soil in Bisset's pond, with its natural bottom, will not freeze solid and the hardy plants will thrive in this environment. However, modern pools do not usually have clay bottoms; instead we use membranes of plastic to contain the water and grow our plants in pots. This means we must have a deeper section to prevent overwintering soil from freezing up and shallower shelf sections for growing plants during the summer.

PUMPS VERSUS STILL WATER

If there is a battle zone in pond construction, it is centered on the use
or avoidance of pumps and moving water in the pond.

MANY WOULD-BE POND KEEPERS are deterred from making a start in this direction under
the impression that running water is necessary, whereas it is really undesirable.

—A. E. HODGE, *Garden Ponds and Pools*

If you think for a moment about where you see water lilies in
nature, they are almost always found in still water. Even if their home
is a river, they are found in a still backwater or quiet section of the
moving water. Water lilies do not like actively moving water, and they
do not grow well when their leaves are jerked around by wave action.
To grow a lily, then, quiet water must be designed into the water pond.

Soils to Use

Just because a water lily soil is out of our sight does not lessen
its importance for growing a good plant and more importantly,
from a gardener's point of view, a large crop of flowers.

NOT A FEW who have attempted, or contemplate, growing aquatics over-look
the great need—absolute necessity—of a very rich soil, and plenty of it, to
have these plants grow successfully.

—WILLIAM TRICKER, *The Water Garden*

A good lily soil should have several characteristics. First, it should be a heavy soil with as much clay in it as possible. Clay soils tended to be richer and provide better flowers than lighter or sandier soils. Never add peat moss or additives such as perlite to the soil; they will float right out of the mix, either winding up on the surface or suspended to cloud the water clarity.

THE BEST SELECTION would be a good turfy loam, from sods cut from a pasture and laid in a pile, adding one-third to one-half well rotted cow manure, stable, or farmyard manure, where a liberal admixture of cow manure is assured, or old hotbed manure, whichever is available.

— WILLIAM TRICKER, *The Water Garden*

The soil should also be fertile. While using manure in the soil mix, as recommended by almost every one of the old-time authors, will create fertility, it will also turn the water brown for the first week or so until the nutrients have been consumed by the algae. Lately, I have been putting the manure or compost on the bottom of the pot in a compacted layer and filling the rest of the pot with soil to cover over this layer. This has reduced but not eliminated the browning. Gardeners with a shorter attention span or a need for immediately clear water would do well to avoid compost and manure; use fertilizer tabs instead.

THE PROPORTION of cow manure to use is one part to six parts loam, and this makes the finest of all planting mediums, but in the event of difficulty in procuring it, a 32 pot of ground bonemeal to a barrowload of loam makes an excellent substitute. Horse and pig manures are useless for aquatic culture.

— FRANCES PERRY, *Water Gardening*

The proportion of compost or manure to use in the soil mix is quite high—ranging between one-sixth to one-half of the mix depending on the author. I note this by way of pointing out that water lilies are very greedy feeders. You may just have to put up with brown water for a short time.

As a last characteristic of good lily soil, remember to avoid sandier soils or sand itself when putting soil into the lily tubs. Some gardeners have reasoned that if sand is good in aquariums, then using it in ponds—which may be seen as simply large aquariums—is similarly acceptable. While sand may work on a small scale, on a larger scale it creates problems. It does not feed the lilies or provide a heavy enough medium for good root development. Lilies planted in sandier soils will constantly float to the surface until they have established a good root system.

Sand is an asset in the aquarium, but we consider it out of place in the outdoor pool. Shun, too, old swamp mud or dredgings from river beds; it is entirely without food value, as witness the heaps of mud often seen by canal banks—with not even the commonest weeds flourishing on them.

— Frances Perry, *Water Gardening*

Feeding

A vigorous water-lily rapidly exhausts available food material in a small receptacle, and if there is no room for expansion, becomes in time weak and starved.

— Frances Perry, *Water Gardening*

CONTAINERS

Modern gardeners, in contrast to the advice from the classic authors and gardeners, use pots that are too small for their lilies. We should be using laundry hamper–sized pots and instead the nurseries are selling half bushel basket–sized containers. Our Mr. Bisset advises us to use oil barrels; while we are not likely to run out to find oil barrels, it does give us some indication of the pot size this turn-of-the-century author would recommend. Tricker, a slightly earlier gardener, recommends that "where a large fountain basin, tank or pond affords ample space for free development, and where flowers of the first size and quality are desired, use shallow boxes, ten to twelve inches deep, and three to four feet square, placed on the bottom" (Tricker 1897). The important point in the last author's note is "where flowers of the first size and quality are desired." If you want large flowers, you have to have large pots. Bigger is better.

IF OIL BARRELS are available, they can be sawn in two, and will answer very well in place of boxes. These barrels should be burned lightly to remove any oil or other deleterious matter remaining of their former contents; they can then be filled with the soil, and carried to their places in the pond.

—PETER BISSET, *The Book of Water Gardening*

Water lilies demand a lot of food if they are to produce a flower a day and if that flower is also going to be of a good size and quality. Frances Perry made this point clearly and well, and while it was made a few sections back under soils, it bears repeating again because many beginning water gardeners miss this point. While plants in the perennial garden can tolerate a lack of fertilizer and still bloom adequately, if you underfeed water lilies they will underperform. If you want dinner-plate-sized leaves and flowers, feed your water lilies.

Modern garden centers sell small fertilizer stakes and tablets, which will do an acceptable job if put into the soil every second week or, at the very least, monthly. The tablets must be buried a few inches deep in the soil or as they melt the nutrients will escape from the soil to dissolve into the pond water, feeding the algae instead of the plant. When I used these tablets, I would push them well down into the soil with my fingers and then tamp the soil back on top of them to prevent their escape.

Wintering in the Pond

If the pond has a natural bottom, overwintering is as simple as watching the frost and ice make their claims on the garden. After the first serious frost knocks back the leaves, clean the pond of all debris. This advice is easier said than done, but it is much more comfortable to clean the pond in the fall when the water still retains some of its warmth than wait until spring and experience the minute difference between frozen ice and spring water temperatures. Cleaning the fall pond also eliminates any excess organic debris that will rot over the winter. Rotting organic matter consumes oxygen and reduces fish survival rates.

THE SOIL WILL have to be dug out to the required depth, which may be from eighteen inches to two to three feet, the depth must be considered in comparison with the normal thickness of ice formed in the locality, for the roots of Water Lilies must not freeze, although they are designated "hardy."

—WILLIAM TRICKER, *The Water Garden*

Tricker points out accurately that water lilies must not freeze. I have frozen the odd one and had it survive, but as a rule of thumb freezing is tantamount to killing. If the pond has a modern membrane or plastic bottom, with a deep section that will not freeze solid, you can lower the water, clean out the pond, and drop the pots into the deep section for overwintering.

After the cleaning of natural-bottomed or plastic-bottomed ponds, you should return the water level to its normal level for the winter. If fish or plants are left in the pond, they will require this water, but even if the pond is to remain barren over the winter, it simply looks better filled up. Some modern authors have recommended leaving the empty pond half filled with water so that snow and spring rains will fill it up again. I have never seen the logic in this nor have I ever seen it recommended by any of the old-time experts.

WINTERING OUT OF THE POND

I winter my hardy plants in an old household freezer. The freezer is located in an unheated shed, the lilies—still in their pots—are stacked inside, and then the freezer is filled with water. I put a cattle trough heater—a large birdbath heater would do as well—inside just to ensure the water does not freeze solid and then I shut the lid and ignore the plants for the winter. In the spring, I siphon out the water with a garden hose, divide the plants, recharge the pots with fresh soil, compost, and drop them back into the pond.

I use the old freezer because I do not have a cold cellar, crawl space, or garage that stays cool but does not freeze. If I had one of those perfect storage areas, I would simply put the pots in black plastic bags and store them in the cool area. Once a month, I would check to ensure they were still wet since drying out will kill a lily faster than freezing will. Bisset seems to agree; in his experience "More roots of hardy lilies are lost every Winter through being kept too dry than by being frozen" (Bisset 1907). If the gardener is growing lilies in tubs without holes, the tubs can be kept topped off with water and no plastic bags are needed.

I do know a gardener who treats his lilies as he cares for his tender roses. He buries both in the ground for the cold winter. While I doubt he has read *The Water Garden*, this advice was printed there in 1897. William Tricker wrote, "The tubs can be wintered in a cellar, or plunged in the ground and covered with leaves, bracken, or any material that will prevent them from freezing." This seems like a lot of work to me, but the technique works well for those who are more inclined to dig holes than store plants in old freezers or cold cellars.

Do not let your lilies freeze and do not let them dry out. These are the two most important points in overwintering water plants. Whatever system you use, if it accomplishes these two objectives, your plants will continue growing and you will quickly require the following section.

PROPAGATING LILIES

Lilies, if fed properly to encourage large leaves and huge flowers and if given ideal sunny conditions in still water, will very quickly outgrow whatever size container they are in. They are rampant growers and if not divided regularly will soon choke themselves out. As soon as the ice is off the ponds in the spring, the plants may be divided. Lift the lily from the pot and wash the dirt from the root. In this way, you can easily see all the new growth points. Leave several inches of tuber on each crown — three to eight inches is good — and cut the crowns from the mass of roots. If you do this in the very early spring, the leaves will not have started to develop.

IN MAY THE OLD PLANT may be lifted, washed free from mud and divided by means of a sharp knife. Each crown should have several inches of tuber attached, and the roots cut back. Surplus leaves should be removed and the root replanted.

— FRANCES PERRY, *Water Gardening*

Some authors, such as Frances Perry (1938), recommend trimming back the roots that are attached to the crown, but I have never done this beyond trimming off any damaged roots.

The more good roots and the healthier the root system, the better the plant will be. I do note that many of the Victorian and Edwardian authors recommended trimming the roots of most plants—trees, shrubs, perennials—when they transplanted them, so the recommendation to trim back water lily roots would not be unusual. But even if it was not unusual advice in the nineteenth century, it is not good advice by today's standards.

Oxygenators and Floating Plants

Floating plants, which drift on the surface of the water without a root system fixed in soil, fulfill several important functions in the pond. They absorb dissolved mineral salts or nutrients from the water. Because they absorb this food, algae cannot feed on it and the growth of algae is restricted. By growing quickly, floating plants also cover the surface of the pond, restricting the sunlight available to algae. This restricted sunlight also reduces the spread of algae.

Submerged aquatic plants, called oxygenators in the nursery trade, produce oxygen as part of the normal respiratory gas exchange. As a class, oxygenators are extremely valuable members of the pond community and serve as front-line troops in the battle against algae formation.

It will be seen that there is a regular exchange of gases on the part of the animals and plants in a pond and it is by securing a balance in this direction that the success of a pond largely depends.

—A. E. Hodge, *Garden Ponds and Pools*

Acting in a similar manner to floating plants, the submerged plants absorb nutrients from the water, making them unavailable to algae and depriving it of food.

There is an ecological balance to the pond that is unique in gardening. The largest soil-based flower bed can support a single plant. While it might appear odd to the garden viewer, the plant will be healthy and grow well in this unusual but acceptable ecology. This is not the case in the water garden. A pond requires a balanced ecology — with adequate surface coverage, oxygenators, plants, wildlife and yes, even algae to keep the water clean and clear. A single plant in the middle of a large pond will quickly turn to green scum, consumed by the unbalanced ecosystem around it. Our predecessors understood this and the rest of the chapter will describe some of their methods for solving problems.

ALGAE

ALGAE AND CONFERVAE of various forms are occasionally troublesome, and though not a "disease" are injurious, being of a low order of plant life, some, parasitical, choke the life out of the plants on which they prey.

— WILLIAM TRICKER, *The Water Garden*

Algae comes in three basic forms in our ponds. Pond gardeners try to avoid two of them while encouraging the third. The first is the dreaded floating algae. This form turns the water green and murky. Unable to see through the water, we blame all our pond problems on the algae. The second type is the angel hair algae, a stringy mass of filamentous algae that clogs up filters and winds itself around plants. Pond gardeners are not enamored of this form, either. The form we want to encourage is the third type, moss algae. This layer of green covers the sidewalls and rocks of ponds and provides as much as 50 percent of the necessary dissolved oxygen in the water. Do not, as one gardener of my acquaintance did, lower the water level once a week to wash off the "disgusting green stuff."

Floating algae occurs for several different reasons:

- There are too many fish in the pond or you are overfeeding the fish. The solution to this seems pretty clear—eliminate some fish and/or stop feeding them so much.
- Not enough surface of the pond is covered with plants. Cover at least 65 percent of the pond surface with plant leaves. Whether these are lily or floating plant leaves, covering this proportion of the pond surface reduces the sunlight to algae. Leaving a pond open to the sunlight simply provides an invitation for the algae to grow.
- There are not enough oxygenating plants in the pond. The rule of thumb that I have always worked with in my ponds is to take the uncovered surface area of the pond and divide it by two. That produces the number of clumps of submerged oxygenators to install in that pond to eliminate algae for the summer season. You can reduce the number of oxygenators by increasing the surface coverage (by growing more lilies or floating plants) but, invariably, if you have an algae problem adding enough oxygenators to an unfiltered pond will solve it.

- There is too much waste on the bottom of the pond. Well, the solution to that seems clear, even to me.
- There are chemical fertilizers in pond — from garden or lawn runoff or improper application of water plant fertilizer tablets (see above for correct method). Overfeeding with Nitrogen will create an algae bloom almost overnight.
- There is an excessive movement of water in the pond without proper filtration. Slow or eliminate the pump or install biological and sediment filtration systems.

Filamentous algae is the long "angel hair" type; it is easily removed by twirling a stick in its midst, then pulling it up and out of the pond. The cause of this algae is normally too much organic matter in the pond, too many dying and decomposing plant leaves and fish mucking about in it all. Tadpoles eat the stuff so this is one reason to love having frogs in your pond. Removing it can be a pleasant occupation on a hot summer day; I note I have had worse problems in my garden than this one.

Moss algae is the good guy, the green slippery stuff on the sidewalls and rocks of the pond. Leave it alone to do its job.

Green scum will form whenever new soil and manure have been added to the pond, the still, warm water having a tendency to promote the growth of this particular algae.

— Peter Bisset, *The Book of Water Gardening*

The last point to be made about algae is that every pond will go green in the spring before the natural ecology gets working.

Mosquitoes, Malaria, and Fish

There are many old tales of ponds and the problems they can cause to human health. The most prevalent one is that ponds are a source of mosquitoes and therefore malaria. In 1901, *The Canadian Horticulturalist* suggested that sunflowers were a sure preventative for malaria. Well, maybe they are . . . although I have yet to find another reference that says so.

A pond at the Agricultural College is one of the prettiest features of the grounds. If the owner has fears of its causing malaria, a plot of sunflowers would be a safeguard, for these plants are a sure preventative for malaria.

—Linus Woolverton, ed., *The Canadian Horticulturalist*

Whether the workers imported from foreign countries in the middle of the nineteenth century to dig canals and lay the railroad lines brought it with them or there was some native American form that has since died out, malaria is not a problem throughout North America today. Malaria is now largely confined to subtropical countries. The concern existed, though, and it is passed along to us a constant supply of information about how to control mosquitoes in ponds.

Many are afraid of malaria and mosquitoes proceeding from a pond unless a continuous stream of water is passing through it; this fear is groundless.

—Peter Bisset, *The Book of Water Gardening*

The easiest way to control mosquitoes is to add a small number of fish to the pond. Common guppies and rosy barbs, available at most pet stores, are ravenous predators of insect larvae while the more frequently used goldfish, koi, and golden orfe will accomplish the same task. Guppies and barbs are excellent for small ponds or container ponds or ponds where the carp-family fish disturb the plants. Both the guppies and barbs will breed in ponds with floating or submerged oxygenator plants. As an added benefit, the smaller, faster guppies and barbs are harder for predators to catch.

THE MOST COMMON MISTAKE is in having more fishes in a pond than its oxygen content can support. In this case, they reveal their distress by coming, gasping, to the surface in an endeavor to obtain oxygen from the atmosphere.

—A. E. HODGE, *Garden Ponds and Pools*

The working rule of thumb for fish in an unfiltered pond is to allow one inch of fish for every square foot of pond surface. I note that some modern books have upped this number to two inches per square foot. If the pond is eight feet by four feet or thirty-two square feet in size, it will support thirty-two inches of fish, for example, four eight-inch fish or thirty-two one-inch fish. Exceeding this guideline will create a situation where the fish are excreting too many nutrients for the oxygenating plants to absorb; algae gets established and will not be eliminated until the ecology is restored. The ecology can be restored by adding extra oxygenating plants—hoping the excess hungry fish will not eat them—by adding a biological filtration system to remove nutrients from the water, or by removing excess fish.

Even my big pond gets a green cast first thing in the spring before the oxygenators start working away. A month into the gardening season and the water has cleared up and I can enjoy my sitting area to the fullest. My big pond—named Dug Lake—is 250 feet long, 60 feet wide, and from two to twelve feet deep, so it takes longer to heat up in the spring than the smaller ornamental ponds. These smaller ponds are normally green only for a week or two before the plants start to work their magic. My advice is to establish the surface coverage, calculate the oxygenator requirements, and develop a keen sense of patience.

PESTS

When compared to the perennial or annual border, it seems that water plants are singularly healthy. There are far fewer problems with them in my garden than with any other form of plant. There are, however, a few interesting pests, described below.

My water plants are regularly infested with aphids. Large numbers of them congregate on the growing tips of water lilies or on any leaf that sticks out of the water and stays dry. I enjoy knocking them off with the hose. There is no need to spray toxic chemicals or get excited. Simply get the garden hose out, turn the nozzle to jet strength, and blow them off. Tricker (1911) recommended tobacco dust as an alternative. Let me remind readers that nicotine (tobacco) is a potent insecticide but is no longer used in the home garden (see page 204 for discussion).

THE SYRINGE OR HOSE should be brought to bear on them when quantities will be washed away if not killed; the plants may also be dusted with tobacco dust, but this makes them very unsightly, and should only be used when other means fail.

— William Tricker, *The Water Garden*

Some garden experts will tell you fish will eat aphids. I find some fish do not care for them but others will eat them. Hungry goldfish are more likely to devour them when you knock them off the plants with your hose but well-fed fish ignore them floating on the surface. Other than the level of feeding, I confess I do not know why some fish ignore them while others treat them as a good snack.

Don't expect your fish to eat the aphids for fish do not care for them.

— R. V. Sawyer and E. Perkins, *Water Gardens and Goldfish*

Sometimes the larval stage of *Hydrocampa proprialis*, or the leaf-cutter bug, will be seen in the pond. This larva cuts two oval pieces (about half an inch long) from leaves and hides between them. These pieces float around the pond while the edges of the pond leaves have a scalloped look. The pest is difficult to eradicate because no spray will work on the larva safely hidden between the two pieces of leaf. The easiest thing to do is net them out and crush them.

Leaf Miner

Occasionally a leaf miner infestation will break out in the pond. This is not common but can do an incredible amount of unsightly damage very quickly. If you see small tracks on the leaf surface, leaf miner is the culprit. The tracks are wandering, zigzag white lines in the green leaf; they result from the feeding of the small larva between the leaf layers. Again, no sprays are effective because the insect is protected between the leaves. The easiest thing to do is trace the line to its end—there will be a small brownish worm there. Squeeze it with your fingers. This is a slow but particularly satisfying way of eliminating a destructive pest in your garden.

IT EATS NARROW LINES in the leaf. Where you have but three or four infected plants roll the insect out of the line in the leaf with your fingers and crush it.

—R. V. SAWYER AND E. PERKINS, *Water Gardens and Goldfish*

Four-Legged Pests

Cats and dogs are great predators of the garden pond. The image of a cat perched on the side of a pond eyeing the big dinner-sized goldfish is well known in garden storytelling. Dogs, particularly retrievers such as mine, believe you have constructed the pond for their exclusive bathing privileges. Sawyer and Perkins (1934) suggest chicken wire to keep dogs out of the garden; they have never met my dog nor, I am afraid, many of the dogs of my water-gardening friends. Training is the only way to keep dogs out of the garden—that and providing an alternative source of water for play.

FROGS AND TADPOLES are of great service and should be encouraged in and around the ponds; these, too, have their enemies, the domestic cat should never be allowed near the tanks, as pussy will surely find out the frogs as well as the fishes, of which she is particularly fond.

—WILLIAM TRICKER, *The Water Garden*

CHAPTER EIGHT

LAWNS

BULLA EST VITA HUMANA

Life's a bubble.

—A BOOK OF SUNDIAL MOTTOES

here are few nicer things on a warm day than to lie down on a spring-thick lawn, stretch out your arms and legs in the classic snow-angel form, and just soak up the sunshine. It is a wonderful feeling and one I ritually engage in every year. Lying down on the lawn defines the end of the muddy season and brings me fully into the height of spring. Soft, green springtime grass is to be treasured after a winter of white, and so treasure it I do.

It seems that our Mr. Rockwell (1935) wrote an excellent little book called *Gardening with Peat Moss*, in which he wrote quite eloquently about the use of peat moss on lawns. His definition of the essentials of a good lawn is still sound and forms a good outline for this chapter. A lawn does indeed require good grading, smooth and uniform surfaces, and a good healthy green color.

THE ESSENTIALS OF A GOOD LAWN are three: it should be correctly graded; it should possess a smooth and uniform surface; and it should remain permanently green.

—FREDERICK F. ROCKWELL, *Gardening with Peat Moss*

Grading

A great principle in laying out the lawns is the old principle of Batty Lang-
ley's (a principle which he himself parodied rather than illustrated) of so
arranging your grounds that everything cannot be seen at once, and that each
turn of the walks excites some fresh interest.

— William Robinson, *The English Flower Garden*

Having the grading properly established means that water
movement over the top of the lawn is properly oriented and also
that the water movement down into the soil is controlled. The
old books were more likely to recommend grading and laying of
drainage tiles to solve lawn problems than modern landscapers.
Lawn surfaces should fall away from the house so that surface
water does not find its way into the basement. While this fact
seems elementary, the number of wet basements during rainy
periods indicates that work needs to be done in this area. Those
who garden at the bottom of hills or in the pathways of water
runoff need to take special precautions with grading to channel
the water around basements and valuable garden plantings.

The laying of an elaborate system of pipe drains will not be dealt with here,
its costliness preventing the average flower gardener adopting it; but even
extremely wet gardens may generally be vastly improved by excavating a deep
pit, or cutting a ditch at the lowest end and running a rough drain toward it by
burying a seam of brick rubble and stones two or three feet below the surface.

— A. J. MacSelf, *Hardy Perennials*

Tile drainage is an expensive solution for wet lawns or gardens, but — and this is a big but — it is a permanent solution to
the problem. It is also less expensive than a constantly wet base-

ment and the problems that accompany it. As a mechanical solution, drainage tile moves the water that is drowning the roots
and allows gardening and lawn establishment on land that
would not previously support good lawns. We had an area of our
garden that was quite swampy every spring and early summer, it
was only after drainage tile was installed there that plants other
than cattails would survive.

SMOOTH AND UNIFORM SURFACES

Rolling the lawn is a suburban tradition every spring. It is clear
that dragging several hundred pounds of rolling water or
lead around the turf will flatten it out quite nicely. What is less
clear is the reason why modern turf experts do not recommend
rolling on established lawns; it compacts the soil. Soil compaction prevents tender grass roots from growing well; it also
reduces drainage and air spaces in the soil. In short, rolling a
suburban lawn creates more harm to the grass plants than good.
Why has it been recommended all these years? Because it gets
rid of the small bumps in the lawn. Most of these small bumps
can be eliminated by a good stiff raking or by the natural set-
tling of the soil during the summer months. So it does not
matter that almost all authors, writing about lawns, recommended lawn rolling. Modern science has shown that on most
turf grass lawns, it is not a good idea for established lawns. Get
out the rake instead.

THE SEASON AFTER WEEDING many persons are discouraged by the luxuriance of
the weeds, and the apparent faint-heartedness of the grass. They must keep

on mowing and rolling patiently. Most of these forward weeds are of sorts that do not survive having their heads cut off half a dozen times; while good lawn grasses fairly laugh and grow fat with decapitation.

— FRANK J. SCOTT, *Beautiful Homes*

SEEDING VERSUS TURF

Smooth lawns are also a function of the turf itself and how many weeds are established in the lawn area. A good turf area will act to retard the growth of weeds and, with some small effort on your part, you can encourage grass, control weeds, and create smooth and uniform lawn.

BUT NINE OUT OF TEN beginners make the great mistake of assuming that the success of the lawn depends almost entirely upon the kind of seed they use. If the results of a first attempt are not successful, then the remedy employed is to try a different seedsman.

— FREDERICK F. ROCKWELL, *Gardening with Peat Moss*

The differences between sowing grass seed and laying down turf, or sod as it is called today, are simple. Seed is slow to establish and must be maintained while it is in its infancy. Sod is fast; a lawn can appear in a few hours and, as long as it is watered sufficiently to encourage the roots to grow, it is initially carefree. Seed is relatively inexpensive; the labor of the householder is not part of the cost equation. With sod, the labor and capitalization of the sod farm is part of the cost of the instant lawn. Weeds must be controlled in seed sowing, while the sod farm has done all this work for the home owner.

To SECURE A GOOD LAWN, a rich soil is as essential as for the kitchen garden. On small grounds the quickest and best way of making a lawn is by turfing. There are few neighborhoods where good turf cannot be obtained in pastures or by roadsides. No better varieties of grass for lawns can be found than those that form the turf of old and closely fed pastures.

— FRANK J. SCOTT, *Beautiful Homes*

The decision to seed or sod comes down to the needs of the individual home owner. Most of us rarely have to make that decision about establishing new lawns. What we do face is the renovation and maintenance of lawns (see below for a spring recipe that will make this chore much easier).

MOWING

"NOTHING," SAYS BACON, "is more pleasant to the eye than green grass nicely shorn."

— HENRY A. BRIGHT, *The English Flower Garden*

"Green grass nicely shorn" is a pleasant sight to the eye, and when it is combined with the tangy smell of freshly mown grass, the lawn becomes a delight to the senses. This delight is not without its debate, however; our modern gardeners disagree just how tall that "nicely shorn" grass should be. I find that the height of the grass depends on several different factors and there is no single answer that will satisfy every gardener. For those who grow their lawn as a labor of love, a short mowing height of 1 inch is fine.

LAWN MOWER

This height assumes the grass is being fed and watered on a regular basis and that no weeds are allowed to grow due to the regular use of herbicides. For those of us with a more cavalier approach—or those who object to the use of lawn chemicals— a height of 2 inches is more appropriate. The higher turf is healthier, the longer blade of grass supporting the roots means a healthier plant—especially if there is a reduced level of chemical support for the turf. A higher, thicker turf suppresses weed establishment on its own; shading the weed seeds so they do not germinate.

THE ADVICE TO PLANT so as to leave sufficient breadth to swing a scythe wherever there is any lawn at all, is none the less useful, though the admirable little hand-mowing machines take the place of a scythe; for a piece of lawn in a place where a scythe cannot swing, is not worth maintaining.

— FRANK J. SCOTT, *Beautiful Homes*

PEST CONTROL

As in many other forms of gardening, the old-time authors had a limited number of controls in place for lawn pests. I suspect that we share many pest problems, but the approach taken by the nineteenth-century gardener was different from our more modern practices.

[To CONTROL ANTS] catch a toad, place it under a dish, box or flower pot over the ant hill. Leave it there for three or four days, according to the number of ants and the capacity of the toad. When you raise the dish you will find the toad waiting to be moved to fresh feeding grounds with not an ant in sight.

— LINUS WOOLVERTON, ED., *The Canadian Horticulturalist*

In most cases, the old authors do not discuss killing lawn pests. I suspect two things were operating. The first is that the actual level of damage was much less than we might see today; the second is that the standards were also lower than we hold necessary in our modern horticultural practices. I suspect the level of damage was much less because the grass plants were not stressed and constantly forced to grow in unnatural ways. The grass was fertilized with manure and allowed to grow quite long. The high level of organic matter, relatively low levels of nitrogen food, and long blade length kept the grass plant healthy and growing well and thus better able to resist pests and diseases than today's chemically fed and short-mown turf. Second, our lawns have become a fetish in modern society—golf-course-green perfection is the standard and anything less is seen as a failure. The lawns of the nineteenth century were not—in any conceivable way—up to this standard of appearance. Nor did the Victorian home owner suffer the angst of having to maintain those impossible standards. Without the pressure to produce a golf-course-standard lawn, pests were—unless they decimated an area—accepted in the course of having a green turf area.

In short, we are left with a dearth of recommendations from our gardening predecessors about lawn pests. This may, in itself, be a message for us to consider. We may choose to revert to their environmentally friendly systems of care, create healthier turf grass areas, and lower our expectations as to what is an appropriate standard for our gardening.

THE WEED SPUD: A GOOD TOOL

I AM NOT IN FAVOUR of using acids or other chemicals to exterminate deep rooted weeds, as the careless or immoderate use of chemicals would probably do more harm than good, in most cases. A constant and vigorous campaign during the summer against these intruders on the lawn with the weed-spud, supplemented by the use of the lawn rake, will in a short time rid the lawn of weeds, if at all carefully done.

—LINUS WOOLVERTON, ED., *The Canadian Horticulturalist*

I inherited a weed spud from my grandfather's toolshed and it is an elegantly simple tool both to describe and to use. The working end is a flat piece of metal approximately two inches wide and ten inches long with a sharpened V-shaped groove cut in one end. The other end of the metal is attached to a long wooden handle. The V groove is placed under the leaves of the weed against the root, and a quick thrust of the handle severs the root. With a bit of practice, the gardener can learn to sever the roots several inches below the soil surface. The effect of this is to force the weed to regrow another top and

WEEDS

If our ancestors were not particularly aware of or bothered by lawn insects, the same is not true for weeds in the lawn. These, they noticed. However, without the chemical arsenal available to modern gardeners, they were left to deal with these problem plants with either physical tools or some crude chemical treatments. The weed spud (see accompanying sidebar) to expend stored energy doing so. Rake the cut up leaves from the lawn. Once the new tops appear, the gardener once again cuts them off with the spud. Repeated several times in the course of a growing season, this will deplete the energy stores of most plants. As long as the gardener does not give up before the plant does, the lawn will slowly become weed-free. A weed spud is less work than aerobic exercise but has no associated club costs, clothing needs, or travel requirements. Weed spuds are used in the comfort and privacy of your own home and yard with only a curious neighbor or two to question your actions. These are only a few of the good reasons why weed spuds should make a comeback.

WEEDS OF CERTAIN SPECIES, however, will persist in thrusting their uninvited heads through the best kept lawns. These are to be dealt with like cancers. A long sharp knife, and busy fingers, are the only cure for them.
—FRANK J. SCOTT, *Beautiful Homes*

was a prominent tool in the garden sheds of those aspiring to good lawn care.

As a final note on weeds, the nineteenth and early twentieth centuries saw gardeners experimenting with using various chemicals and "treatments" for the eradication of lawn weeds. These treatments ranged from the simple-but-effective (such as pouring boiling water on pathways) to the extreme (polluting garden areas with acids and petroleum products to discourage weeds and insects). On the whole, however, the weed spud and a sharp knife were the treatments of choice.

A CORRESPONDENT WRITES that he has used Gillett's lye for destroying weeds and grass that grow up in gravel walks and through slats, with success. He says, "A fairly strong solution should be made and poured carefully between the slats, and in a day or two all the unsightly grass and weeds will have disappeared."

— LINUS WOOLVERTON, ED., *The Canadian Horticulturalist*

Recipe for Spring Care

ON LAWNS, WHERE for reasons, such as the scarcity of water, or perhaps imperfect under-drainage, the sod becomes thin and weak growth, weeds of all kinds are sure to appear.

— LINUS WOOLVERTON, ED., *The Canadian Horticulturalist*

In 1901, *The Canadian Horticulturalist* noted that a thin lawn was an invitation to weed seeds and that they were "sure to appear." I have been using the following recipe for several years with good success to thicken up the lawn and stop the growth of weeds. For every one thousand square feet of lawn area, spread a four-cubic-foot bale of peat moss (more is acceptable), one bushel of compost or equivalent (two bags the size normally found in garden centers is equivalent), and two pounds of grass seed over the area. If the lawn is very thin, add extra grass seed — going up to as much as four pounds if necessary. Do this every spring. If the lawn is in the shade and the grass is struggling,

routinely add three pounds of seed every spring. The objective
is to add extra organic matter from the peat moss, minor nutrients from the compost, and extra grass to thicken up the turf to
shade out developing weeds.

ONE REASON WHY we should take care to get the best turf which the conditions
of soil or climate allow is that no other country but ours can have such good
turf. In many countries even in Europe, they cannot have it at all, but grass
seed has to be sown every year to get some semblance of turf.

— WILLIAM ROBINSON, *The English Flower Garden*

While my lawn would never be mistaken for a golf course green, it is a serviceable surface on which my children, our pets, and I play with regularity and great enjoyment. Having adjusted my attitude to resonate with that of my gardening teachers, I find myself enjoying myself much more and relaxing into the tasks of lawn care rather than battling for each individual blade of perfection. I suspect this is why I will never qualify as a golf course greenskeeper.

WATERING THE LAWN

ONE WOULD THINK that watering a little garden is quite a simple thing, especially if one has a hose. It will soon be clear that until it has been tamed a hose is an extraordinarily evasive and dangerous beast, for it contorts itself, it jumps, it wriggles, it makes puddles of water, and dives with delight into the mess it has made; then it goes for the man who is going to use it and coils itself round his legs; you must hold it down with your foot, and then it rears and twists around your waist and neck, and while you are fighting with it as with a cobra, the monster turns up its brass mouth and projects a mighty stream of water through the windows on to the curtains which have been recently hung.

—KAREL CAPEK, *The Gardener's Year*

Lawn grass is quite succulent stuff and this lushness demands regular watering. On average, it takes between one and two inches of water a week to keep a lawn looking good but, for the most part, this was beyond the technological abilities of our gardening ancestors to accomplish. Pushing large quantities of water demands water pressure and water pressure was only available via motorized pumps for crops of some commercial value—if even then. Lawns had to survive with what nature provided. We have family pictures of our early beginnings on the farm with the front lawn—a renovated pasture—turning quite brown in the heat of July and August to green up again with the rains of September.

Now that we treat water pressure as a fact of life, we can lay out the sprinklers to keep the lawns green. By applying the one to two inches of water in one or at most two applications in a week, you ensure the lawn will develop deep roots and will stay lush for the summer. The easiest way to accomplish this is to measure how long it takes the sprinkler to put one inch of water in a measuring tub or pail. Time the sprinkler for this length of time for the weekly watering to ensure adequate coverage. The rule of thumb is that the application of the one inch of water on sandy soils is divided into two applications, while regular or more claylike soils receive the water in a single weekly dose.

FEEDING THE LAWN

There is no question that our gardening predecessors treated their lawns as they treated any other form of gardening. If they wanted it to grow, they applied manure or compost. Not only did they apply manure, they applied it in great amounts.

BEFORE WINTER BEGINS all newly laid turf should be covered with a few inches of manure. The manure will have protected the grass from the injurious effect of sudden freezing and thawing in the winter and early spring and the rich washings from it gives additional color and vigor to the lawn the whole season. This fall manuring is essential to newly set turf, and is scarcely less beneficial if repeated every year.

— Frank J. Scott, *Beautiful Homes*

Scott ([1870] 1886) went as far as suggesting a few inches of manure be laid down every fall, to feed and protect the turf. I am not sure how urban neighbors would react to a few inches of fresh manure in the fall, but I am certain the turf grass would be very appreciative.

Modern gardeners are not likely to apply manure to the lawn in large quantities so they are reduced to supplying organic matter with peat moss and compost (see above spring recipe) and using other ingredients to feed their lawns. Our Mr. Scott ([1870] 1886) also recommends "cold soap suds" as a good summer feed for lawns. I suspect this real soap — not detergent — would have high levels of potash from the wood lye used in its manufacture.

Cold soap suds applied from a sprinkling-pot or garden-hose when rains are abundant, is the finest of summer manure for grass.

— Frank J. Scott, *Beautiful Homes*

I suppose gardeners can save their soap suds and pour these over their lawns but I suspect, once again, that many readers will not undertake this level of technology.

We are left then to ask just what is it that modern gardeners can do to feed their lawn and when is a good time to do it. Downing (1854) has part of the answer when he says that "as early as possible in the spring" is the best time to feed the lawn. The rest of the answer comes from research at the University of

Guelph; they recommend the following program for feeding low maintenance lawns. The amount of nitrogen to be used through the growing season is two pounds for every one thousand square feet of lawn, a half pound very early in the spring, followed by a half pound in late June or very early July. The third application should be a full pound in late October after the grass is dormant but before the soil freezes. This is a reduced amount from that normally recommended by lawn care companies but is sufficient to keep the grass growing well without creating a lush expanse beloved of insects and diseases. Note that the amount of nitrogen is not the amount of fertilizer. The amount of fertilizer to be applied depends on the analysis of the product. If the analysis is 35-10-15 (35 percent nitrogen, 10 percent phosphorus, 15 percent potash), then the fertilizer contains roughly one-third nitrogen. It will take one and one half pounds of fertilizer to provide half a pound of nitrogen.

As EARLY AS POSSIBLE in the spring is the best time to apply such a top-dressing, which may be a compost of any decayed vegetable or animal matter—heavier and more abounding with marsh mud, etc., just in proportion to the natural lightness of the soil."

—ANDREW J. DOWNING, *Landscape Gardening*

CLEAN STABLE MANURE, fine and rotten, is about the best all round fertilizer for the lawn, and the effect in the rich, dark green growth is very soon observable. If this is not convenient, excellent results may be obtained by sowing the lawn 1) with wood ashes, at the rate of from 25–50 bushels to the acre, to furnish potash, an important element in the formation of the stems and woody portions of vegetation; 2) with nitrate of soda, say 75 lbs to the acre, to promote vigorous growth; 3) with bone meal, about 200 lbs per acre, which aids the nutrition of the plant.

—LINUS WOOLVERTON, ED., *The Canadian Horticulturalist*

Those with a desire to experiment may want to follow the advice of *The Canadian Horticulturalist* (1901). It recommended wood ash, nitrate of soda, and bone meal as alternatives to manure. I note that this amount of wood ash works out, roughly, to a maximum of one bushel of wood ash for every thousand square feet of lawn. Those with fireplaces may find this useful information. Excess wood ash will alter the acidity of the soil, making it more alkaline, and reduce the growth rate of grass plants. Apply bone meal at four and one half pounds per thousand square feet to meet these recommendations. Nitrate of soda—the nitrogen in the recipe—might be a little harder to come across in our modern world. Nitrate of soda is Chilean saltpeter, and is not to be confused with our modern saltpeter, which is potassium nitrate. Modern garden centers do not stock either of these products nor, I suspect, will they in the immediate future.

As a last note to lawn feeding, modern gardeners feed lawns several times a year. Andrew J. Downing ([1871] 1886) speaks for the nineteenth-century authors when he recommends, "Where a piece of land is long kept in lawn, it must have an occasional top-dressing every two or three years, if the soil is rich, or every season, if it is poor."

Chapter Nine

Vegetables

ver non semper virit

Spring is not always green.

— A Book of Sundial Mottoes

ometimes, when I ask the old fellows visiting our
nursery how their gardens were last year, they
respond with "Oh, I don't garden anymore, I
just put in a few flowers here and there." The first
few times I got this response I was a bit confused,
but finally it dawned on me that to these old farmers the "garden" meant the vegetable garden. A few flowers didn't count as
true gardening. This was 180 degrees from my flower-nursery

training and I confess, hearing the response always brought a smile to my day. However upon reflection these gardeners were not far off the mark. Every spring we spend almost as much time and effort picking the vegetables for the garden as we would spend time choosing flowers for the entire nursery. My wife and I would also "discuss" the kinds of tomatoes we each wanted to grow; mine were chosen for the speed of growth, size, taste or newness for trial while she chose hers for the canning speed and lack of moisture in the jar.

THERE ARE SEVERAL different ways in which to lay out a little garden; the best way is to get a gardener.

    —KAREL CAPEK, *The Gardener's Year*

    Sometimes though, I ask myself, "Why am I doing all this?" It is a lot of work, too much stooping in the hot sun, and boating on some faraway summer shore looks very good. Liberty Hyde Bailey ([1915] 1980), the eminent plantsman, put it this way: "To farm well, to provide well; to produce it oneself; to be independent of trade, so far as this is possible in the furnishing of the table: these are good elements in living." Putting in a garden is a good element of living, and each winter when I enjoy the canned tomatoes—following their direct route from my garden to my saucepot—I have to agree with the old fellows and be glad I am still gardening.

GARDEN MARKER

Planting and Sowing

The techniques for improving the soil of the vegetable garden have been covered in the chapter on soil (see Chapter 1). In
my own gardens, however, I have followed for the past twenty
years a pattern that is not mentioned in the old books but
has worked well for me.

I operate the vegetable garden on a three-year cycle. The
first year, I lay a heavy mulch of straw down over the entire garden. I use straw because it is available from local farmers, but
any available and inexpensive mulch would do equally well. The
straw bales are broken up for the plant rows but only "flaked" off
for the walking rows. The flakes—a compressed bale of straw
comes apart in layers—are more dense, and they make a surface
that is easy to walk on and push the wheelbarrow across instead
of the fluffed-up plant areas. A flake of three to four inches thick
makes an excellent organic paving stone. The plant areas are
fluffed up to twelve to eighteen inches thick to better enable me
to move the mulch around the base of plants or pull it aside to
create areas where seeds will be put directly into the ground.
These planting areas will settle over the summer into a good
layer of easily moved or handled mulch. Not only do I mulch
heavily but I also compost equally heavily, following the recommendations of Peter Henderson ([1866] 1895) to apply four
pounds of compost per square foot (see Chapter 1).

In year two, the garden is composted again but no new
mulch is laid down. The old mulch is still intact and doing
a good job. In year three, I compost in the spring as normal

SEED CATALOGS

The essence of seed catalogs has not changed all that much in the past hundred years. The prose is still excessive, the descriptions fantastic, and the desire they create overwhelming. Colored pictures have replaced the woodcuts but that only increases the temptation to overspend and overplant—as if overplanting was even a remote possibility in my fantasy garden!

APPROACHING ARE THE DAYS of the seed catalogues! By the patriotic housewife they are hailed with joyous acclaim—that is, both the days and the catalogues—for they are harbingers of greater production.

   —E. C. RANDOLPH, in *Everywoman's World*, FEBRUARY 1918

A good vegetable seed catalog not only entices unwary gardeners to try the latest and best-tasting varieties but provides information about the numbers of seed in each package as well as the cultural details needed to succeed with each individual crop. I see this information as just reward for my overindulgence in seed every year. And, as Randolph (1918) so aptly put it, these seed catalogs are the "harbingers of greater production." I rarely get as heavy or as good-looking a crop in August as I do in my January dreams. Find your catalogs through the Internet, in gardening magazines, and by word of mouth from friends. I never met a gardening catalog I would not browse.

CABBAGE SEED WILL GERMINATE freely when four years old, if it has been well preserved. To keep seeds sound they must be kept dry.

   —DELORS W. BEADLE, *Canadian Fruit, Flower, and Kitchen Gardener*

One problem that some new garden-ers express about catalog gardening is that they always have excess seeds after their small gardens are filled. Many new gardeners question whether they can store these excess seeds. Happily, the answer to this is a resounding yes; I store most vegetable seeds for several years—saving money in the process—by putting the excess in a regular envelope and keeping it in a small shoebox in the crisper of the refrigerator. As long as the seed name is on the label and ravenous teenag-ers do not mistake the seeds for snacks, most seeds will be fine for sev-eral years of storage. Excess seed from too much enthusiasm for catalogs is not wasted in my garden. Keep those seeds cool and dry and they will easily survive for a year or two.

BRUSSEL SPROUTS

AMONG THOSE ONLY SAFE for two years are: Beans and Peas of all kinds, Peppers, Car-rot, Corn, Egg Plant, Okra, Salsify, Thyme, Sage, and Rhubarb. Those safe for three years: Asparagus, Endive, Lettuce, Parsley, Spinach, and Radish. Those safe for five years: Broccoli, Cauliflower, Cabbage, Celery, and Turnip. Those possessing the greatest vitality are: Beet, Cucumber, Melon, Pumpkin, Squash, and Tomato; the time ranging from six to ten years.

—PETER HENDERSON, *Gardening for Profit*

and garden all summer, but in the fall, as the mulch is starting to get a bit thin in places, I till the remaining straw into the soil. The following year, I start the process all over again with a heavy layer of straw mulch.

BROCCOLI: IT IS SAID to be more hardy than the Cauliflower, and on that account can be left out all winter in places where the winters are mild, but as we never have such winters in Canada, this difference has no practical existence here.

—DELORS W. BEADLE, *Canadian Fruit, Flower, and Kitchen Gardener*

There are two points to be made about this practice. The first is that mulch is available to even the most urban of gardeners. There is no reason why newspaper—with its vegetable-based inks—cannot be shredded and recycled into the vegetable garden. Tree leaves are an excellent vegetable garden mulch. Even coarse wood shavings—available in country-suburban feed stores specializing in horse needs—can be used as a surface mulch. The local electrical utility work crews often dump their wood chips at our place, which I have used quite successfully over the years as mulch on top of the straw. As long as the plants are being fed properly, the wood chips—contrary to garden myths—do not create a problem in the vegetable garden.

The second point is that by using a three-year rotation of mulch, it is easy to create a three-year garden crop rotation. With the garden split into three sections, it is easier to remember that the tomatoes go over into the far west end in year one, the center in year two and the far east in year three. No crop is

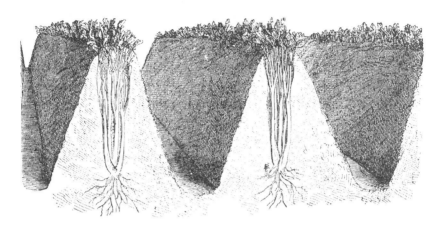

CELERY, EARTHED UP

ever grown in the same place two years in a row. This may not be careful planning as Randolph (1918) would have us do, but it is easy and makes life easy for us real gardeners.

THE GARDEN WHICH IS CAREFULLY PLANNED will give a greater yield, a more even distribution of products, and provides more generally for winter requirements without any increase in expense or work than the garden planted without any definite plan.

—E. C. RANDOLPH, IN *Everywoman's World*, FEBRUARY 1918

GETTING AHEAD OF THE SEASON

Getting ahead of the season, being the first on the block with new peas or early tomatoes is a competitive gardener's dream. Even Thomas Jefferson (1944) engaged in early pea-growing competitions with his friends and once proved his merit as a scholar and gentleman by refusing to announce his winning crop to dampen the enthusiasm of his friend and regular winner, George Divers.

No, SAY NOTHING ABOUT IT, it will be more agreeable to our friend to think that he never fails.

— THOMAS JEFFERSON, *Garden Book*, 1766–1824

A good friend of mine always puts his early pea crop into the ground on the Easter weekend. This may have something to do with his status as a retired clergyman, but more likely it concerns his gardener's desire to be able to announce the first pea crop in our area.

While peas will take a lot of cold weather and abuse, most vegetable transplants will be set back by cooler weather. Remember that soil temperatures are the most important variable in getting a good start to vegetable seedlings. The higher the soil temperature, the faster and more reliably the plant grows. The old and very likely apocryphal story of the old farmer dropping his pants to sit on the warming soil each spring to test its readiness for planting is not likely to be copied by many urban gardeners. It is duly noted that the back of the hand is almost equally as temperature sensitive as that more nether region of our anatomy, and if the back of the hand can be left comfortably on the soil surface, it is time to plant tender vegetables.

THE TREE AND VINE in ones own garden abundantly fruitful through ones own attentive care! No fruit so sweet, no vegetable so tender, no flower so fine in

color or so fragrant as those from our own garden. Every mother owns the
finest baby in all the world and every gardener grows the finest produce. Loving care assures this miracle.

— E. H. WILSON, *If I Were to Make a Garden*

Some gardeners like to push the season—using various
means and methods. Before the age of plastics, gardeners used
various methods, with the cold frame being the most common.
Modern gardeners can also use cold frames; I used to regularly
enclose the seedlings with straw bales and cover the enclosure
with a sheet of plastic to protect my tender seedlings. A rectan-
gle constructed of one-by-eight planks covered with plastic
would do the same. The newer plastic frost-fabrics are equally
effective and easily available. It seems the older I get, though, the
less likely I am to resort to this kind of subterfuge. I garden more
in tune with the season and if the back of my hand is not warm
enough, the seedlings do not go in. To be sure, I may not have
the earliest tomato or pepper plants in the region, but I do get
the best-tasting, least-stressed-out plants from a much less
stressed-out gardener.

To really beat the season in your neighborhood, follow
this tip. As soon as the snow is gone from your garden, lay
a sheet of clear plastic over the area you wish to use early. Tuck
the edges down into the soil so that no breeze can penetrate
under the plastic. A trench works best and most elegantly for
this but wooden two-by-fours held down with heavy cement
blocks will suffice. This is a greenhouse in its most simple form,
and it will act as an unvented solar collector to trap heat in the

soil. Trapped heat is the secret to early success. Within two weeks the ground inside the trench will be covered with all the tiny weed seedlings normally found much later in the season. To really warm the soil *and* knock the weed crop back, pull back the plastic and rototill down the weeds. Reinstall the plastic. The warmer soil has been tilled under, pulling cooler soil to the top. Wait another two weeks; the soil under the protected plastic will be much warmer than the surrounding soil—particularly the neighbors'—and almost ready for planting. Remove the plastic, rototill to knock back any new weed seeds, and work in the compost. Planting time has arrived.

We doubt, however, if on the whole it pays our farmers to provide the necessary hot-beds and sash required to grow a crop of very early Tomatoes, because such are the facilities for transportation in these early days of steam, that the more southern grower supplies the earliest Tomatoes in spite of all we can do.

—Delors W. Beadle, *Canadian Fruit, Flower, and Kitchen Gardener*

Does this mean that your planting time is earlier than in the neighbors' gardens? Likely not. Both vegetable gardens can be seeded at the same time, but the one with the warmer soil will germinate seeds faster—or establish plants faster if you use transplants—and the plants will grow faster, with no setback caused by cold soil, and will yield earlier. Warm soil is the key to good growth and early yields. Warm soil, however, will not stop air frosts from blackening the transplants, so if a frost is due plant protection is a must.

We had not peas nor strawberries here till the 8th day of this month. On the same day I heard the first whip-poor-will whistle. . . . Take notice hereafter whether the whip-poor-will always come with the strawberries and peas.
— Thomas Jefferson, *Garden Book,* 1766–1824

Remove the clear plastic sheet just before planting or sowing seeds. If you do not remove the plastic, the heat under it will continue to build up during the summer until it kills or stunts the roots of the vegetables. Leaving clear plastic on over the entire summer is an excellent method of solarizing the soil and clearing it of weeds and weed seeds. If solarizing, please remember that early growth under the clear plastic will be phenomenal; weeds will grow to sizes never before imagined. Have patience—a month into the real heat of the summer all those huge weeds will be fried under the heat of the firmly tucked-in plastic solar collector.

Black plastic does not warm the soil as quickly as the clear variety but can be left on for most of the summer in cooler areas. It also retards the germination of weed seeds because sunlight is not available to initiate it. Cover black plastic with organic mulch in hotter areas at summer's height. The organic mulch will stop the plastic from collecting too much heat and stunting vegetable growth. Even though the black plastic creates a high heat zone, it does not create enough heat for solarization; use clear plastic for that.

GREEN GLOBE
ARTICHOKE

Weeds

Many of us forget that gardeners of earlier times had never heard of herbicides. In almost every gardening book I own, this advice—or something too similar to mention—is included: "Weeds will now begin to appear plentifully, from seed, in every part of the garden. The utmost diligence should be used to destroy them while they are young, before they get the start of the crops; especially towards the middle and latter end of this month, when, if a forward season, they will be advancing in rapid growth (Mawe and Abercrombie n.d.). The "utmost diligence" is a key phrase that still holds true today in our gardens. The old-timers in our area say that "One year's weed sows seven more." A word to the wise is enough and a word to the foolish is one too many. Use "utmost diligence" in your garden if weeds are not to ruin your plot of ground.

On the other hand, sometimes the best of intentions are simply that—intentions—and the weeds win the battle. Boiling water is a simple yet effective solution to most perennial weeds, and it kills them quickly. I remember my mother with a kettle of water, pouring it onto the cracks in the patio stones in our home garden. The roots of dandelions were cooked and killed in front of my eyes, leaving the patio weed-free for another few months. I have used this technique successfully myself on our own stone walkways, and I find that the more slowly I can pour the water over the weed, the more effective the treatment. The dandelions wilt within a few minutes and die off within the day. This slow method is fine for limited areas, but it would take

STIRRING OF THE SOIL

Beadle (1872) wrote about cabbage fertilization: "Frequent stirring of the soil is exceedingly beneficial to the cabbage, and an abundant supply of well rotted manure essential to the attainment of best results. Ashes and lime are excellent manures for the cabbage, and best of all finely-ground bones, at the rate of a ton to the acre, sown broadcast on the ploughed ground and harrowed in." While scattering a ton of old bones around the garden might not be the best way to endear ourselves to the neighbors, applying bone meal ("finely-ground bones") as a source of phosphorus is a well-established gardening principle. I note that Beadle suggested harrowing the bones into the soil. This is consistent with modern gardening knowledge that tells us that phosphorus is not readily water soluble and does not easily move downward in the soil. We know to put our phosphorus source (usually bone meal) deep into the soil where it is readily available to plant roots. Scattering it around the surface effectively removes it from being useful to the plant and is a waste of bone meal and the money it cost.

too much water to get ahead of a weed infestation in an entire garden; serious weed infestations only respond to the more labor-intensive system.

For those who do not mulch—my solution to weeds—and whose gardens regularly fill with plant pests, there is an organic

solution to weed control emerging to save the day. Turn to page
53 to discover the wonders of corn gluten.

DISEASES

Something that never fails to amaze me is the difference
between discussions of plant diseases in the old gardening texts
and those in more recent books. The vintage texts only discuss
the very common problems, normally associated with insects,
and rarely discuss physiological diseases and bacterial or viral
agents. Now, there are two possible explanations for this. The
first is that our forebears' science was not advanced enough to
tell them they had a bacterial or viral problem; the second is that
they did not have the same level of problems that we face today.

There is no question that the science of today can identify
and catalog more diseases than could our gardening ancestors in
the seventeenth through nineteenth centuries. On the other
hand, there is no question that our ancestors were better at the
fundamentals of gardening than we are today. They had the
basics of plant health down cold; they dug well, they composted
and manured copiously, and they spaced their plants regularly.

THE CARELESS AND UNTHINKING cultivator will, in the end, be driven from
the field by the man who uses his brains and makes himself informed upon
the best modes of culture, and studies the requirements of his soil and of the
plants he cultivates.

— DELORS W. BEADLE, *Canadian Fruit, Flower, and Kitchen Gardener*

Digging allowed plant roots to expand and grow in a healthy
way; one can argue that plant health begins at the very bottom

with a good root system. Compost, as we have seen in Chapter I, breaks down into humus, and humus has been demonstrated to have curative effects on plants and negative effects on some soil-borne plant problems such as nematodes. Well-composted soil is healthy soil. Adequate plant spacing allows air circulation to dry off leaves after dewy mornings, and dry leaves do not support bacterial colonies. Adequate spacing also leaves the plants without the stress of competition for food and water. Reducing the stress on our plants will have the same effects as reducing the stress on ourselves — they (and we) will have better, healthier, and stronger growth and maintenance systems. Combining all three of these conditions in a single garden allows plants to grow with a reduced chance of major diseases striking.

On a personal note, I have been gardening organically for twenty years and rarely see the problems my more chemically oriented friends and customers see in their gardens. I have to agree with Delors Beadle (1872), in the very first Canadian gardening book, when he expressed the sentiment that the best man or gardener would be one who "studies the requirements of his soil and of the plants he cultivates."

Did plant problems strike the old-time gardeners? One only has to examine the Irish Potato famines to know the all-too-harsh reality that they indeed existed.

I HAVE BEEN A WORKER of the soil since my boyhood, and every year's experience convinces me of the almost helplessness of remedies against insects or other blighting plagues that attack vegetation in the open field. It is true that the amateur gardener may save his dozen

BEAN

or two of cabbages or roses by daily picking off or destroying the insects; but when it comes to broad acres, I much doubt if ever any remedy will be found to be practicable, unless in rare instances, such as Paris Green, as an antidote against the Potato Bug. We have one consolation, in knowing that these pests are only periodical, and never continue so as to permanently destroy."

— PETER HENDERSON, *Gardening For Profit*

Peter Henderson has stated the problem quite nicely I think. On the broader farm scale, problems exist that may indeed "blight" the crops in the field. Commercial agriculture already knows that "Paris Green" was not, and is not, an all-time antidote for the potato bug. With resistance to chemicals on the increase, there are no permanent cures for pests or diseases. Luckily, on the "amateur gardener" scale, it is possible to control problems by a variety of environmentally sound means. I also continue to take heart from Henderson assurances that all the problems are only periodical and if I persevere, these problems will not permanently destroy my garden.

WITH SOIL THOROUGHLY UNDER-DRAINED, well and deeply pulverized, and abundantly supplied with manures, the foundation is laid for successful gardening.

— DELORS W. BEADLE, *Canadian Fruit, Flower, and Kitchen Gardener*

PESTS

Insect control in our ancestors' gardens was often mechanical rather than chemical. Early gardeners used water sprays to knock aphids from the plants, and they transferred the techniques from the garden to the house or container plant (see above for disease control techniques). Sometimes though, commercial gardeners tried things almost out of desperation to avoid a crop and financial loss. Peter Quin, in his *Money in the Garden* (1871), which was aimed at commercial growers, suggested that "Dusting the plants, when they first come through the surface, with flour of bone, and repeating it after each rain" would control the elusive flea beetle. This tiny black beetle chews small holes in plant leaves; the gardener rarely sees it because the slightest disturbance of the plant canopy causes it to leap off the plant. Its existence is diagnosed by holes in the leaf rather than actually sighting the insects. Henderson ([1866] 1895) similarly recommends bone meal for keeping the cabbage caterpillar under control. He also suggests dusting with lime to achieve the same results. Lime and bone meal were used by many of the commercial gardeners and subsequently, home gardeners, as cures for a variety of garden problems.

ANOTHER EXCELLENT REMEDY is to steep, at the time of sowing the seed, ten or twelve pounds of tobacco-stems in a large tub, adding three or four quarts of soft-soap and some urine. When the plants are up and any signs of the "fleas" appear, the bed may be syringed with this tobacco solution, and the plants dusted with some air-slacked lime.

—PETER T. QUIN, *Money in the Garden*

Another technique, still used today, is using tobacco or nicotine as a powerful insecticide. I note that nicotine smoke is a controlled greenhouse substance in our controlled-chemical agricultural regulations, with an LD50 rating of 50. This makes it an extremely dangerous product and one that requires oxygen-supplied respirators for safe use. In comparison, Diazanon, a commonly available pesticide, has a moderately dangerous LD50 rating of 300, while Ambush, a synthetic pyrethrum that is similarly used on aphids and other soft-bodied pests, has an LD50 rating of more than 4,000. (Higher is better!) Nicotine smoke and sprays are potent chemicals! Quin and his contemporaries did not burn the tobacco; they made a tea out of it (Quin 1871). A common recipe for the times, recommended by multiple authors, is to steep tobacco stems to create a liquid insect poison.

This is not recommended for modern gardeners as nicotine is a potent insecticide and toxin!

IF YOU COAT THE CUT ENDS of the branches with a mixture of rat droppings and sulphur, and then lightly apply a hot iron to this, the new growth will diminish and appear normal.

—DAVID A. SLAWSON, *Secret Teachings in the Art of Japanese Gardens*

Just because a technique is old, it is not necessarily either good or beneficial. Soaking tobacco stems for vegetable sprays should be treated the same as the use of rat's dung in a mix to paint on tree wounds. They are both interesting relics of our common history but not recommended for modern gardeners.

Reference List

Amateur Cultivator's Guide to the Flower and Kitchen Garden. 1845. Boston: Washburn and Co.

Bailey, Liberty Hyde. 1910. *The Nursery Book.* 14th ed. New York: Macmillan Co.

———. [1915.] 1980. *The Holy Earth.* Reprint, New York: Scribner's.

———. 1925. *Manual of Gardening.* 12th ed. New York: Macmillan Co.

Beadle, Delors W. 1872. *Canadian Fruit, Flower, and Kitchen Gardener.* Toronto: James Campbell and Son.

Biles, Roy E. 1950. *The Complete Book of Garden Magic.* Chicago: J. G. Ferguson.

Bisset, Peter. 1907. *The Book of Water Gardening.* New York: A. T. De La Mare Co., Ltd.

Bright, Henry A. 1881. *The English Flower Garden.* London: Macmillan and Co.

Capek, Karel. 1951. *The Gardener's Year.* 14th ed. London: Allen & Unwin, Ltd.

Crane, Howard. 1963. *Gardening on Clay*. London: W. H. & L. Collingridge.

Cutting, A. B. 1938. *Canadian Home Gardening the Year Round*. Toronto: Musson Book Co., Ltd.

Downing, Andrew J. [1859.] 1967. *A Treatise on the Theory and Practice of Landscape Gardening*. 6th ed. Reprint, New York: Funk and Wagnalls.

Farrer, Reginald. 1928. *The English Rock Garden*. 4th impression. London: T. C. and E. C. Jack, Ltd.

"Garden Calendar." *Organic Gardening Magazine* (September 1948): 47.

Heinrich, Julius. 1911. *The Window Flower Garden*. New York: Orange Judd.

Henderson, Peter. 1895. *Gardening for Profit*. New York: Orange Judd.

Hodge, A. E. 1939. *Garden Ponds and Pools*. 2nd ed. London: H. F. & G. Witherby, Ltd.

Hubbard, S. C. 1926. *Roses and Their Culture*. New York: Orange Judd.

King, Mrs. Francis. 1927. *The Flower Garden Day by Day*. New York: Frederick A. Stokes.

Jefferson, Thomas. 1944. *Garden Book 1766–1824*. Philadelphia: Independence Square.

Loudon, Jane. [1843.] 1851. *Gardening for Ladies and Companion to the Flower Garden*, edited by Andrew J. Downing. Reprint, New York: John Wiley.

Macoun, John, and H. B. Spotton. 1879. *The Elements of Structural Botany*. Toronto: W. J. Gage and Co.

MacSelf, A. J. 1932. *Hardy Perennials*. London: Thornton Butterworth, Ltd.

Mawe, Thomas, and John Abercrombie. n.d. *The Complete Gardener*, edited and revised by George Glenny. London: William Tegg.

Park, Geo[rge] W. 1900. *Park's Floral Guide 1900*. Libonia, PA: George W. Park.

Parkinson, John. [1629.] 1907. *A Garden of Pleasant Flowers*, edited by A. H. Hyatt. Reprint, London: T. N. Foulis.

Perry, Frances. 1938. *Water Gardening*. London: Country Life, Ltd.

———. 1955. *The Woman Gardener*. New York: Farrar, Straus and Cudahy.

Quin, Peter T. 1871. *Money in the Garden*. New York: Orange Judd.

Rand, Edward Sprague, Jr. 1866. *Bulbs: A Treatise on Hardy and Tender Bulbs and Tubers*. Boston: J. E. Tilton and Co.

Randolph, E. C. "The War Garden and How to Plant It to Effect Best Results." *Everywoman's World* (February 1918): 11.

Reid, John. [1683] 1907. *The Scots Gard'ner*. London: T. N. Foulis.

Robinson, William. 1905. *The English Flower Garden*. 9th edition. London: John Murray.

Rockwell, Frederick F. 1930. *The Home Gardener Handbook: Roses*. New York: Macmillan Co.

——. 1935. *Gardening with Peat Moss*. Boston: Bruce Humphries, Inc.

Sackville-West, Vita. 1955. *More for Your Garden*. London: Michael Joseph.

Sawyer, R., and E. Perkins. 1934. *Water Gardens and Goldfish*. New York: A. T. De La Mare Co., Ltd.

Scott, Frank J. [1870.] 1886. *Beautiful Homes: The Art of Beautifying Suburban Home Grounds*. New York: John B. Alden.

Shelton, Louise. 1915. *Continuous Bloom in America*. New York: Charles Scribner's Sons.

Slawson, David A. 1987. *Secret Teachings in the Art of Japanese Gardens*. New York: Kodansha International, Ltd.

Tricker, William. 1897. *The Water Garden*. New York: A. T. De La Mare Co., Ltd.

Warner, Charles Dudley. 1885. *My Summer in a Garden*. Boston: Houghton, Mifflin, and Co.

Wilson, E. H. 1931. *If I Were to Make a Garden*. Boston: Stratford Co.

Woodcock, H., Drysdale, K. C.; and J. Coutts, V. M. H. 1935. *Lilies: Their Culture and Management*. London: Country Life, Ltd.

Woolverton, Linus, ed. 1901. *The Canadian Horticulturalist*. Grimsby, Ontario: 1901.